Cambridge Elements ≡

Elements in Cognitive Linguistics
edited by
Sarah Duffy
Northumbria University
Nick Riches
Newcastle University

NAVIGATING THE REALITIES OF METAPHOR AND PSYCHOTHERAPY RESEARCH

Dennis Tay
The Hong Kong Polytechnic University

CAMBRIDGE
UNIVERSITY PRESS

CAMBRIDGE
UNIVERSITY PRESS

Shaftesbury Road, Cambridge CB2 8EA, United Kingdom

One Liberty Plaza, 20th Floor, New York, NY 10006, USA

477 Williamstown Road, Port Melbourne, VIC 3207, Australia

314–321, 3rd Floor, Plot 3, Splendor Forum, Jasola District Centre,
New Delhi – 110025, India

103 Penang Road, #05–06/07, Visioncrest Commercial, Singapore 238467

Cambridge University Press is part of Cambridge University Press & Assessment,
a department of the University of Cambridge.

We share the University's mission to contribute to society through the pursuit of
education, learning and research at the highest international levels of excellence.

www.cambridge.org
Information on this title: www.cambridge.org/9781108971485

DOI: 10.1017/9781108975049

First published 2022

A catalogue record for this publication is available from the British Library.

ISBN 978-1-108-97148-5 Paperback
ISSN 2633-3325 (online)
ISSN 2633-3317 (print)

Navigating the Realities of Metaphor and Psychotherapy Research

Elements in Cognitive Linguistics

DOI: 10.1017/9781108975049
First published online: November 2022

Dennis Tay
The Hong Kong Polytechnic University
Author for correspondence: Dennis Tay, dennis.tay@polyu.edu.hk

Abstract: The 'real-world' commitment of cognitive linguistics is demonstrated by increasingly extensive collaboration between researchers and industry partners. Yet, there has been little critical reflection on the lessons learned from these collaborative efforts. Beginning researchers may benefit from in-depth discussion of how various practical realities inform, constrain, or otherwise shape important methodological and/or analytic decisions. This Element reflects on long-term collaborative work between a metaphor researcher and psychotherapists, offering practical advice on navigating the latent realities of this type of research. The three foundational components of psychotherapy – the therapist, the client, and the interactional setting itself – are discussed in turn, covering issues such as ethically engaging therapists in research design and data analysis, dealing with underexplored variabilities in client responses, and managing the inherent tension between spontaneity and control in an interactional setting like psychotherapy. Some thoughts on how the lessons are transferable to other research contexts are offered.

This Element also has a video abstract: www.cambridge.org/navigatingrealities

Keywords: metaphor, psychotherapy, collaborative research, practitioner engagement, client responses

ISBNs: 9781108971485 (PB), 9781108975049 (OC)
ISSNs: 2633-3325 (online), 2633-3317 (print)

Contents

1 Introduction

Cognitive linguistics commits to a usage-based approach to linguistic structure, meaning, acquisition, and change (Barlow & Kemmer, 2002; Evans & Green, 2006). This broadly means that cognitive linguistic theories are based upon observed language use rather than the unobservable mental mechanisms that characterized previous dominant paradigms. At the same time, cognitive linguists are increasingly taking steps to show the practical applicability of their work in contexts ranging from education to advertising and health. Both commitments are related in that they advocate serious engagement with the 'real world' beyond what is inside the heads of linguists and language users. They also imply that insights from cognitive linguistic research should not only aim to benefit the social world, but should themselves be based upon careful consideration of the characteristics and constraints imposed by real-world research settings.

This real-world orientation of cognitive linguistics has been demonstrated in many different ways. They range from theoretical discussion of the sociocultural groundings of cognition and language (Frank, 2008; Geeraerts et al., 2010) to extensive collaboration with practitioners and other stakeholders in different domains of application (Demjén & Semino, 2020; Littlemore & Turner, 2019; Pérez Sobrino et al., 2021). Collaboration with industry and societal partners is an increasingly important avenue to demonstrate innovation, vision, and research impact in the humanities and social sciences. From an educational perspective, such efforts generate a wealth of experience, knowledge, and skills that could help less experienced researchers plan similar initiatives. However, there has not been much space dedicated to critical reflection and discussion of these lessons learned and how they bear implications for basic research assumptions and practices. Practical questions, such as how to synergize the expertise of linguists and domain experts, or how methodologies and analyses are constrained or enabled by the inherent features of social activities, are seldom posed and answered. The present work aims to exemplify such reflective discussion in a focused context by drawing upon my engagement with mental health professionals and clients in projects investigating the uses of and responses to metaphors in psychotherapy. Metaphor is a mainstay of cognitive linguistics research, implying that a good number of metaphor researchers are trained in linguistics. Research on metaphors in mental healthcare settings has not been as widespread as in other domains of social activity, such as education and advertising. Nevertheless, it is an excellent example of a social activity where different practical realities – the characteristics of therapists and clients, and the spontaneous interactional setting of psychotherapy – have to be carefully navigated by metaphor researchers in order to make the most of opportunities and avoid pitfalls. Before outlining these realities, we first review the major motivations for wanting to understand metaphors in psychotherapy.

1.1 Researching and Applying Metaphors in Psychotherapy

Conceptual metaphor theory (CMT) (Lakoff, 1993) is widely recognized as the preeminent theory of metaphor in cognitive linguistics, and it continues to be developed in different directions to the present day (Kövecses, 2020; Steen, 2011). The following central claims of CMT will already be familiar to readers who know cognitive linguistics, but will serve as a useful introduction otherwise:

- Metaphorical expressions pervade everyday language.
- Clusters of related metaphorical expressions reflect coherent metaphorical thought patterns.
- Metaphorical thought patterns can shape our attitudes and behaviors.

The claim that metaphorical expressions pervade everyday language is a radical one. It departs from the traditional and more intuitive view that metaphors deviate from 'normal' language to serve ornamental functions (Grice, 1975). Proponents of CMT point out that mundane expressions such as *I am in love* and *she is moving up the ranks* are in fact subtly and irreducibly metaphorical. In *I am in love*, the feeling of love is described as being physically 'in' some implied container. Likewise, in *she is moving up the ranks*, the notion of achievement is described as physical upward movement. These are metaphorical because, barring exceptional circumstances, lovers are not actually in containers and achievers are not actually moving upward. They are furthermore irreducible in that it is difficult to think of natural but nonmetaphorical ways to replace them. The remarkable fact is that similar expressions exist across different languages and cultures (Kövecses, 2005; Yu, 1998) and also manifest in nonverbal forms of communication (Forceville & Urios-Aparisi, 2009) – imagine, for example, a cartoon depicting someone with a briefcase climbing up a 'corporate ladder.' Besides, these are not isolated or one-off examples because speakers can readily conjure up a near-infinite number of creative expressions that reflect and extend the same metaphorical links. Someone *moving up the ranks* may *stumble and fall* and require someone else to *pull her up* again, and when we *fall out of love* we know not to *dig such a deep hole* for ourselves the next time. Such meaningfully patterned expressions point to an underlying cognitive mechanism whereby more abstract ideas (e.g., love, achievement) are made sense of in terms of more concrete physical experiences (e.g., space, movement), and logical inferences are made on that basis. Numerous other examples exist, including depicting desire in terms of hunger, anger in terms of heat, and so on (Lakoff & Johnson, 1999). These cognitive mechanisms are called 'conceptual metaphors,' each consisting of a 'target domain' (the thing that is conceptualized) that is systematically mapped onto a 'source domain' (the thing used to conceptualize the target). Much debate centers around whether conceptual metaphors are psychologically real and coherent thought patterns, or just superficial generalizations of language (Gibbs, 1996; Glucksberg, 2003). Lastly, perhaps the most intriguing and controversial CMT claim is that conceptual metaphors have the power to shape our attitudes and behaviors. Ways of thinking and acting that cohere with certain metaphors are more likely to be seen as natural or acceptable, which might further sanction them as guides for future action (Lakoff & Johnson, 1980). For example, English speakers conventionally describe arguments as metaphorical warfare (*he shot down my arguments; this is a crossfire session*). This could naturalize physical aggression as a way to settle disputes, and metaphors could thus be exploited as strategies to construct one social reality over another (Musolff, 2012). Framing studies have indeed shown that metaphorically couched policies on immigration and health care exert significant effects on audience evaluations in ways that are consistent with the source domains (Boeynaems et al., 2017).

The three aforementioned claims establish a far-reaching inferential chain linking language to thought and social action. Despite criticisms of circularity, reductionism, and insensitivity to sociocultural realities (Anderson, 2003; McGlone, 2007; Murphy, 1997; Quinn, 1991), CMT has been an indispensable underlying theoretical framework in many applications of metaphor research for the benefit of social activities such as education, advertising, and health (Low et al., 2010). One area that is claimed to resonate particularly well with CMT's conceptual and behavioral claims is the mental-health practice of psychotherapy (Wickman et al., 1999). A popular definition of psychotherapy is the

> application of clinical methods and interpersonal stances derived from established psychological principles for the purpose of assisting people to modify their behaviors, cognitions, emotions, and/or other personal characteristics in directions that the participants deem desirable. (Norcross, 1990, p. 218–220).

Metaphors have interested therapists throughout the history of the practice, though not always in their linguistic form. They play a significant role in Sigmund Freud's influential theory of dreams, wherein the content of dreams is thought to symbolize unconscious motivations and desires (Edelson, 1983).

The relevance of CMT for many therapists is even more apparent because it shares their key concern with the relationship between language, thought, and human behavior. Therapists and clients use words to describe issues, explain concepts, and build a therapeutic alliance during their encounters. Language, in fact, almost fully constitutes treatment delivery and processes, which gives psychotherapy its nickname: 'the talking cure.' Furthermore, potentially problematic behaviors, cognitions, emotions, and/or other personal characteristics are often difficult to describe in literal terms, so people rely on metaphors and other figurative devices to express them (McMullen, 2008). This has been observed in traditional face-to-face and more innovative forms of mental e-health alike (Tay, 2015). Consider the following exchange, with noteworthy metaphorical expressions underlined:

> Client: I'm super, super sensitive the last four or five days. I haven't been around people much, and it's kind of purposeful, I think. I just don't want to be around them because I don't really feel like talking and because, well, they are something other than – it's fun to talk to them when I've <u>got my act together</u>, but when I don't, it's like it <u>takes my mind away</u> from what I'm doing. And I've had enough trouble, I don't want to <u>lose track</u> of it anymore. But I was noticing on the way home that, from one song on the radio to the next, my mood <u>shifts</u>, sometimes almost <u>180 degrees</u>. And it's like, <u>the way I am right now</u>, just the slightest little thing can change my emotions. It's like a <u>feather in a rapid stream</u>, which I don't like. I hate the <u>instability</u> of it. And yet, there doesn't seem to be any <u>way</u> I can <u>solidify</u> my emotions. Because the more I concentrate on them, the more likely I am to <u>force</u> them <u>to move rapidly in one direction or another</u>.
>
> Therapist: Now there's something frightening about being so vulnerable to being affected by <u>outside things</u>. Like talking to somebody else, or a song <u>shifting</u> you. (Tay, 2017e, p. 371)

It would be quite challenging for the client to express his complicated feelings in purely literal terms without losing some nuances in meaning or at least sounding awkward. "A feather in a rapid stream," for example, seems difficult to translate into concise nonmetaphorical language. The therapist likewise chooses to build upon the client's metaphor in his response by acknowledging how being "shifted" by a song shows his vulnerability. Major paradigms, such as cognitive behavioral therapy (CBT) (Beck, 1976) and others influenced by constructivist philosophy (Neimeyer & Mahoney, 1995), are further aligned with CMT on the idea that such metaphors are not mere linguistic descriptions but reflect active construal of clients' subjective realities. Exponents of CMT might, for instance, claim that even a somewhat conventional expression like "outside things," which is metaphorical because it describes a state of affairs in terms of a physical location, has the potential to be exploited for therapeutically relevant purposes, such as providing a coherent frame to discuss the client's state of affairs. In general, metaphors can provide important clues on the client cognitions that are deigned to underlie their mental and behavioral issues (Tay, 2017b). Some major theoretical developments in CMT continue to bear relevance for therapists. The 'discourse dynamics' approach (Cameron & Maslen, 2010), for example, argues that conceptual metaphors are not fixed structures tied to specific words, but dynamically unfold across complex interactional sequences of the type often seen in psychotherapy. Deliberate metaphor theory (DMT) (Steen, 2011) is another development which focuses on when, how, and why speakers explicitly draw their listeners' attention to the use of conceptual metaphors – psychotherapy being a prime example where this is common (Tay, 2016a). Compare, for instance, "I am a feather in a rapid stream" with "I often imagine I am a feather in a rapid stream."

The aforementioned considerations have led to a blossoming of research on the use and management of metaphors in psychotherapy. Therapists have identified key functions of metaphors, including relationship building, accessing and symbolizing client emotions, uncovering and challenging clients' tacit assumptions, working with client resistance, and introducing new frames of reference (Cirillo & Crider, 1995; Lyddon et al., 2001). Linguists, on the other hand, have documented the characteristics of metaphors in psychotherapy and their implications for linguistic theory (Ferrara, 1994; Tay, 2013). While some believe therapists should prepare metaphors to explain things to clients (Blenkiron, 2010; Stott et al., 2010), others advocate working with spontaneous client metaphors, as in the example quoted earlier, with guidelines to develop them collaboratively (Kopp & Craw, 1998; Sims, 2003; Tay, 2012). Therapists working with culturally diverse populations further point out the benefits of using culture-specific resources such as religious scriptures as a source for inspiring metaphors (Dwairy, 1999). The influence of metaphors on treatment processes and outcomes has also been observed in more empirical ways. Creative metaphors are linked with deeper reflection and engagement (Gelo & Mergenthaler, 2012), and good outcomes are associated with the ability to transform negative metaphors (e.g., "carrying the burden") into positive ones ("unloading the burden") as sessions progress (Levitt et al., 2000; Sarpavaara & Koski-Jännes, 2013).

It seems, then, that psychotherapy is an excellent context for applied metaphor research, which requires meaningful collaboration between linguists and mental health practitioners. Many therapists have tended to understand metaphors differently than linguists (Edelson, 1983; Lankton & Lankton, 1983), as a psychological rather than linguistic or cognitive phenomenon. It is encouraging to witness the increasing recognition and use of linguistic theories and methods in the psychotherapy literature, including fundamentals such as metaphor identification (Mathieson et al., 2015b; Spong, 2010; Törneke, 2017; Wickman et al., 1999). Concrete collaborative outcomes between linguists and therapists are also increasing, one example being a recent special issue of the journal *Metaphor and the Social World* on metaphor in mental health care (Tay, 2020b). It is time to share with less experienced linguists that researching metaphors in psychotherapy, or anywhere else, involves much more than simply transposing existing theoretical know-how to a new setting. We must also consider how stakeholders' knowledge, expectations, variabilities, and the opportunities and constraints inherent in real-world settings influence our decisions as metaphor researchers. In a nutshell, we must "expand (our) theoretical perspectives to account for empirical data" (Gibbs, 2010, p. 3). Section 1.2 moves beyond the specific case of metaphor in therapy to provide a broad overview of how contemporary collaborative research is conceptualized. It situates our specific case as just one example of the many opportunities and challenges open to language and metaphor researchers. We will return thereafter to a focused discussion of the psychotherapy context, represented by its three foundational components: the therapist, the client, and the interactional setting between them.

1.2 The Dynamics and Ethics of Contemporary Collaborative Research

The limitations of an intuitive 'research-into-practice' model, which separates knowledge production by researchers from subsequent implementation by industry partners, has led to critical reflection on how collaborative research should be carried out (Nyström et al., 2018). Indeed, today's collaborative landscape between linguists and nonacademic stakeholders is more diverse than ever before, and is limited to neither (mental) health care contexts – 'practitioners' in the conventional sense – nor the fairly specific type of collaborative dynamic to be featured in this work. There are many examples beyond health care where collaborative research is performed and constantly reflected upon. A cursory list includes the traditional domain of language education (Bucholtz, 2021), modern forms of media and advertising (Pérez Sobrino et al., 2021), and forensic sciences (Coulthard, 2010). We will revisit some of these examples in the concluding section of this work.

Martin (2010) details a useful framework to conceptualize the collaborative relationship in terms of five ordered categories, along which we see a trade-off between what he calls "practitioner engagement" and "academic independence." None of these categories are claimed to be superior; they are meant to introduce novice researchers to the lay of the land and guide them toward a collaborative dynamic that best suits their circumstances. The categories are, in increasing levels of engagement and decreasing academic independence, the practitioner as *informant, recipient, endorser, commissioner*, and *core-searcher.* We may briefly consider these categories in the context of linguistics research. Practitioners who are 'mere' informants do not contribute to funding or research design, but mainly perform roles such as gatekeeping information. As pointed out in Section 1.3, this reflects the conception of therapists as little more than session transcript providers. The trade-off is minimal threat to academic independence and minimal political or ethical risks. Some of the risks that accompany increased practitioner engagement will be discussed in Section 2. Practitioners as recipients have research findings actively disseminated to them through various channels and knowledge transfer activities. These may raise awareness but fail to target current practice or policy agendas because practitioners "become involved only on the academics' terms" (Martin, 2010, p. 214). When the research field itself is still budding – for example, in the case of forensic linguistics – this might be the most common collaborative dynamic. Practitioners as endorsers and commissioners have far greater influence in research priorities, directions, and appraisal. The key difference is that endorsers do not pledge funding and therefore have "nothing to lose" in supporting promising research projects (Martin, 2010, p. 215), while commissioners initiate and fund projects to serve their nonacademic interests. This gain in influence implicates political and ethical issues that go beyond the research to the collaborative relationship itself, such as authorship, data ownership, interference in the research process, and unclear differences in ethical conventions across cultures (Morris, 2015). The relationship is also likely to become more complex and pluralized in that other stakeholders – patients, community members, and so on – become centrally involved. Collaboration with therapists is a case in point because issues related to clients cannot be overlooked, as is shown in this work. As more and more linguists are invited or commissioned to participate in collaborative projects, these issues will be of increasing concern. The final category sees practitioners as coresearchers working closely with researchers throughout the project. This is quite literal in medical contexts, wherein practitioners and even patients may temporarily commit themselves full time (Marks et al., 2018). While such full-time commitment is less common in linguistics research, it is at this level that we anticipate fully cocreative and coparticipatory processes wherein practitioners and researchers synergize their expertise. The case to be presented in this work is but one instance among other fascinating examples, such as designing effective marketing strategies (Pérez Sobrino et al., 2021), health care promotional materials (Semino et al., 2018), and revitalizing heritage languages in the community (Furbee & Stanley, 2002). All of these diverse areas share the common potential to inspire new collaborative pathways and possibilities. Regardless of the research area(s) and collaborative dynamic(s) envisioned by a researcher, virtually all funding bodies and ethical review boards today expect a transparent account of how roles and responsibilities will be distributed among the team, as well as an evaluation of the potential risks to all involved parties. More specific examples of these will be discussed in Sections 2 and 3. For a more focused discussion of ethics, work by Bos (2020) and Israel (2015) may be especially helpful to guide early researchers.

1.3 Three Foundational Components of Psychotherapy: The Therapist, the Client, and the Interactional Setting

Regardless of whether they are also active researchers, therapists are usually a direct point of contact in a collaborative project. A major barrier to collaboration has always been the obvious and important issue of client confidentiality. Therapists are obliged to ensure that what is said in the therapy room stays there. Nevertheless, those open to collaborative research are often willing to take steps to obtain data with informed consent or in ways that do not undermine the confidentiality of their clients. This can be seen from the increasing number of well-regulated online databases of transcribed therapy talk for general training and research purposes. An excellent example is the *Counseling and Psychotherapy Transcripts* database (https://search .alexanderstreet.com/counseling-therapy) published by Alexander Street Press, a growing collection of nearly 4,000 anonymized session transcripts featuring different therapy approaches. The high incidence of unfortunate events in recent years that have disrupted mental well-being on a large scale, such as social unrests and the COVID-19 pandemic, has also led to collaborative projects of various kinds. From personal experience during the 2010 earthquakes in Christchurch, New Zealand, therapists offering free or heavily subsidized services to the community found it easier to obtain informed consent to research their spoken interaction with clients as a gesture of reciprocity. Although therapists perform the obvious and indispensable role of 'data providers,' this is fast becoming inadequate in view of growing expectations about what research impact in the humanities entails. The onus is on linguists to convince potential collaborators and funding agencies alike of the value of our intended research. A big part of this comes from finding ways to engage therapists along the research trajectory in ways that go beyond merely providing data.

As a brief example, consider the following (translated) utterance from a female, middle-aged, Chinese client (Tay, 2016c). She had been experiencing severe conflicts with her son and ex-husband. She was frustrated at failing to help her son with his own psychological issues, and angry at her ex-husband for not making a similar effort:

> 在帮儿子之余，我要做好我自己。那我现在肯定不会想在我儿子生病当中，对我父亲，有我父亲的遗憾。我不想再次出现在我儿子的身上。这也是我为什么让他去北京去治疗。As I help my son, I want to take care of myself. I certainly do not want to feel the regret I have towards my father over my son's illness. I do not want it to appear again on my son. This is why I sent him to Beijing for treatment.

Imagine a linguist analyzing this utterance without input from a therapist. They might rely on (i) lexical-level metaphor identification procedures, like MIP(VU) (Pragglejaz Group, 2007; Steen et al., 2010), and determine that words such as "towards" and "appear" are metaphorical; (ii) discourse-level procedures, like the discourse dynamics approach (Cameron & Maslen, 2010), and determine that phrases such as "appear again on my son" are metaphor vehicle terms; or (iii) conceptual-level approaches, like CMT, and posit something like REGRET IS AN OBJECT as a conceptual metaphor operating in the client's mind. However, it is unclear how any of these approaches would connect with what most therapists would see as the most striking feature, which is that the client is displaying transferential behavior. This means the subconscious tendency to project past relationships and experiences onto present ones as a result of unresolved feelings, attitudes, and behaviors (Grant & Crawley, 2002). Conversely, a therapist working this case might entirely overlook how such behavior leaves behind useful linguistic traces. It was sustained discussion, intersecting both observations, that brought the insight that transferential behavior could be modeled as the highly generic conceptual metaphor PRESENT IS PAST. Furthermore, the linguistic instantiations of this metaphor go beyond what would be identified as metaphorically used words under linguistic procedures like the aforementioned MIP(VU). An example is the phrase "I do not want it to appear again," where the only word clearly related to the PRESENT/PAST domains is "again," and the bulk of the metaphoricity is carried by the overall context of use. We will discuss in greater detail this type of collaborative analysis, as well as other forms of meaningful engagement with therapists, such as collaborative experimental/stimulus design, and therapists as experimental confederates.

We then move our attention from therapists to clients. Given the prior focus on therapist–researcher collaboration, one might expect a corresponding account of client–researcher collaboration, which has emerged as a new trend in medical research contexts. Examples include the use of information technologies to engage patients in more intimate and diverse ways than as 'participants' or 'subjects' (Hamakawa et al., 2021; Javaid et al., 2016). The situation in psychotherapy is somewhat different, however, as the sensitive nature of mental health issues often precludes comparable levels of client engagement with research. The present emphasis will therefore be placed on an important issue with underexplored implications for how we approach metaphor research in therapy: that of individual variability in client attitudes and responses to metaphors. While it seems obvious that no two clients, therapists, and dyads could ever be exactly alike (Wohl, 1989), theoretical tensions between universality and cultural/individual specificity have long existed in psychotherapy, as well as in cognitive linguistic and metaphor research. Conceptual metaphor theory started out with a universalist slant by highlighting the invariant aspects of primary metaphors and image schemas (Grady, 1997; Johnson, 1987; Lakoff & Johnson, 1999), but subsequent work has argued for the importance of acknowledging, as well as explicitly modeling, how individuals vary in their metaphor production and comprehension (Demjén & Semino, 2020; Fuoli & Hart, 2018; Kövecses, 2020). This is of particular importance in psychotherapy since clients' expectations, beliefs, attitudes, etc., toward treatment are linked to outcome quality across different paradigms (Greenberg et al., 2006). Furthermore, acknowledgment of client variability manifests the 'patient-centeredness' ideal that is deemed crucial for quality healthcare (Mead & Bower, 2000). Laine and Davidoff (1996) describe patient-centered care as "closely congruent with, and responsive to patients' wants, needs and preferences" (p. 152). Specific to the psychotherapy context, Rogers (1986) advocates the similar view that clients can consciously and rationally decide what works best for themselves, and that therapists should treat different perspectives with empathy and "unconditional positive regard." Different attitudes and responses toward metaphors could thus be seen as an aspect of clients' wants, needs, and preferences. Researchers accustomed to the received wisdom that metaphors 'work' should therefore be prepared for client comments such as "this (metaphor) is all psychobabble to me" and "why use metaphors when you can just say things directly?," and the attendant critical implications. We will discuss how variability in responses to metaphor manifests both consciously and unconsciously in different types of data, including surveys, psychophysiological measures, and therapist–client talk. We will also consider methodological and analytical approaches that can model such variability in an explicit way.

After discussing therapists and clients, Section 4 turns to the constraints imposed and the opportunities afforded by the psychotherapy setting itself. The practice of psychotherapy could be described as a balancing act between spontaneity and control. On the one hand, as defined earlier, it is a type of verbal interaction that is supposed to move "in directions that the participants deem desirable" (Norcross, 1990, pp. 218), which implies a high degree of spontaneity since therapists cannot and should not always predict what clients talk about beforehand. On the other hand, for it to be recognized as an evidence-based healthcare practice, the effectiveness of various techniques and interventions needs to be demonstrated in ways acknowledged by the wider scientific community, such as randomized controlled trials (Dyer & Joseph, 2006). Existing approaches to metaphor research might sit somewhat uncomfortably between these ends. While spontaneous therapist–client talk lends itself nicely to topics such as the interactional and discursive coconstruction of metaphors (Cameron & Maslen, 2010), the findings and implications of such studies are less likely to be considered as exemplifying 'evidence-based' research. Conversely, attempts to compare metaphor (versus nonmetaphor) use between carefully sampled client groups by regimenting what people say would be an obvious violation of the fundamental definition of psychotherapy. This dilemma will be addressed by discussing examples of plausible 'middle path approaches' in research design and analysis that could maintain the balancing act, such that the findings and implications of metaphor research can still be interpreted in meaningful ways from both sides.

1.4 Aims and Objectives of this Work

This work aims to both reflect on lessons learned and impart advice to beginning researchers. It therefore has a more pedagogical orientation than other titles on the use and management of metaphors in psychotherapy, which understandably focus on techniques and their avowed effectiveness. Its two specific objectives are, firstly, to document practical, methodological, and analytical issues that arise from engagement with therapists, clients, and the therapeutic settings they constitute. The second objective is to offer under-explored perspectives and solutions to these issues, which could serve as a guide for researchers invested in similar collaborative work. The discussion stems from just one area of research and is primarily intended for metaphor researchers working within the domain of mental healthcare. Nevertheless, it is hoped that other readers might discover useful general principles that inform their own endeavors in different contexts. Some suggestions are made in this regard in the concluding section by drawing parallels between psychotherapy, education, and advertising.

All of the ideas, examples, and analyses presented in this work have been accumulated over long-term collaborative work with practicing psychotherapists in different settings. I am especially indebted to colleagues from the Mental Health Education and Counseling Centre (MHECC) in Huaqiao University, China, who provided a valuable platform for discussion and knowledge sharing between linguistic researchers and therapists, and great support in data collection and communication with their student clients. The joint research conducted with MHECC was supported by a General Research Fund from the Hong Kong Research Grants Council. Ethics approval was obtained and standard guidelines on informed consent, anonymity, and other relevant aspects were strictly followed.

2 Engaging Therapists as Collaborators

As mentioned in the Introduction, many therapists are in principle willing to collaborate on research if there is reason to believe that the outcomes benefit clients. Linguists can facilitate this by building common ground in the understanding of theoretical constructs, being more aware of the limits of our expertise, appreciating the role of metaphors in therapeutic processes, and balancing the (at times) conflicting ideals of research and clinical realities. This section will discuss how linguists can better engage therapists in three relevant aspects along a typical research trajectory, from designing materials to conducting experimental trials and analyzing data. The discussions tap upon my personal experiences of collaborative projects with practicing therapists, mostly in a university setting working with student clients. The first part uses the example of a client survey on metaphor functions (Tay, 2020c) to illustrate how linguists and therapists can collaborate on stimulus design by combining linguistic expertise in survey construction with clinically informed judgment of its external validity. We then consider the delicate issue of using therapists as confederates to examine client responses to metaphor in actual therapy sessions, which allows linguists to tap upon their clinical expertise in a more direct way. While this may pose ethical questions and is at odds with the ethno-methodological nature of most psychotherapy language research (Peräkylä et al., 2011), some level of control is inevitable if we want to systematically compare the processes and outcomes of language-related interventions. Using examples of recent studies on how metaphorical versus nonmetaphorical communication styles influence clients' affective responses (Tay, 2020a; Tay et al., 2019), we consider how best to mitigate and manage these ethical risks (Kuhlen & Brennan, 2013). Lastly, the possibility of engaging therapists in the analysis of linguistic data is discussed, through a general approach known as 'correspondent analysis' (Tay, 2016c). This involves superimposing or intersecting two independent sets of observations from the linguist and the therapist, as a systematic and replicable procedure to identify areas for further collaborative analysis and theorization.

2.1 Collaborating on Stimulus Design

One of the most common methods in psychotherapy research is the survey. They are often conducted with clients before and/or after treatment to investigate their feelings toward therapeutic processes, outcomes, and other elements. Examples include overall satisfaction (Attkisson & Zwick, 1982), attitudes toward treatment options (Moradveisi et al., 2014), and even beliefs about the nature of their illnesses (Foulks et al., 1986). Incidentally, while the potential functions of metaphors from therapists' perspectives are a common topic in the psychotherapy literature (Cirillo & Crider, 1995; Lyddon et al., 2001), there has been little research on how actual or prospective clients feel about their use, including their performance of such functions. This represents a collaborative opportunity for linguists who should be familiar with surveys as a methodology to investigate attitudes and beliefs related to linguistic elements such as metaphor. At this stage, a plausible research objective that a linguist might independently formulate is to elicit ratings on metaphorical utterances in therapy with respect to the claimed functions in the literature, ideally in systematic comparison with nonmetaphorical equivalents.

An example of a useful source that does not demand specialist knowledge of psychotherapy is Lyddon et al. (2001). It summarizes previous work and argues for the role of metaphors in facilitating developmental change processes in psychotherapy, essentially outlining their key functions. These are paraphrased as (i) building a collaborative relationship, (ii) expressing emotions and experiences, (iii) explaining difficult concepts, (iv) introducing new frames of reference, and (v) working through client resistance. Therapists' sensitivity and awareness to clients' metaphors helps develop a unique shared language and collaborative bond between them. At the same time, such metaphors help "translate the intangibles of emotion (and other experiences) into some sort of verbal expression" (Carlsen, 1996, p. 350). Metaphors also help therapists explain things that may be relatively difficult for clients, such as mental health concepts and the latter's tacit assumptions and worldviews. Relatedly, they can trigger dramatic shifts in perspective and reduce resistance by encouraging clients to think/talk in indirect terms and hence "simultaneously keep and reveal a secret" (Caruth & Ekstein, 1966, p. 38). A point easy to overlook is that the five functions do not necessarily need to be performed by metaphors. They can also be performed using literal language, and it is not immediately obvious that metaphors are the better way of performing them. This is an empirical question that boils down to how therapeutic processes and outcomes unfolding under contrasting linguistic conditions are perceived.

The linguist now faces two important survey design tasks that should no longer be handled independently, but by close collaboration with an experienced therapist. The first is stimulus construction: how to present metaphorical versus literal 'ways' of performing these functions, not just in systematic but therapeutically realistic or externally valid ways. From personal experience of conducting workshops with therapists where the ostensible goal is to 'apply' linguistic research findings to practice (e.g., Tay, 2012), a common feedback was that taken-for-granted constructs such as sources, targets, and cross-domain mappings are often deemed to be too theoretical and "not suitable for everyday use." Therapists interested in metaphors are instead more accustomed to working with examples embedded within actual therapy talk – be it with real or role-played clients with similar profiles as the former (Van Parys & Rober, 2013). This is readily apparent from the writings of some of the staunchest advocates of metaphor use who are themselves therapists (e.g., Dwairy, 2009; Kopp & Craw, 1998; Stott et al., 2010). Many would advise the use of clinical vignettes in this situation – either constructed or reconstructed from prior experience – as a means to embed and compare linguistic techniques such as metaphor and elicit ratings about them. Professional input from therapists would be ideal, if not necessary, for constructing such vignettes. The second task is to formulate the actual survey items to measure each function as a construct. That is to say, what are the key indicators for a general function such as 'building a collaborative relationship' that are considered important from the therapist's perspective? Since respondents would be evaluating these items based on the stimulus vignettes, the two tasks are fundamentally interrelated.

My collaborative plan leading to the results reported in Tay (2020c) involves the therapist first sketching a tentative vignette lasting several turns. Linguistic details, including what and where metaphors appear, are less important at this stage. Instead, the therapist draws from professional experience to create a brief exchange and, most importantly, indicate where each of the functions are enacted. Once this is done, the linguist then exercises discourse/conversation analytic acumen to modify the dialogue and identify sections where metaphors could be introduced without fundamentally changing its meaning. While it might be ideal to have just one overarching conceptual metaphor with one linguistic instantiation per function, this is not strictly necessary since respondents could be assumed to evaluate the vignette in a holistic manner. After checking with the therapist that this 'embellished' vignette with embedded metaphors is realistic from a clinical viewpoint, the linguist then works on a literal equivalent controlling for length, sentence structure, etc. The final steps to ensure comparability involve (i) rechecking with the therapist that both versions are functionally equivalent with metaphorical versus literal language as the only key difference, and (ii) conducting a norming exercise with native Chinese speakers to ensure that both vignettes do not differ significantly along key variables, such as understandability, naturalness, and meaning similarity (Cardillo et al., 2010).

Table 1 shows the final product of this collaborative process. The therapist's initial tentative sketch was based on the typical scenario of students with stress-induced anxiety worried about falling behind others, and how therapists attempt to enact the functions. The linguist identified the first six turns as 'introductory,' and branched off into (i) a literal exchange, and (ii) a metaphorical exchange with 'mountain climbing' and 'artwork' as embedded sources. Both vignettes were then affirmed by the therapist as well as the norming exercise.

After the stimulus is constructed, the therapist's critical involvement continues for the next task of formulating the actual survey items. This requires professional judgment of not only valid indicators that could reflect the function at hand, but also from the perspective of a client experiencing and evaluating the treatment. The collaborative plan is generally similar as noted earlier, with the therapist first drafting a pool of items, the linguist modifying them for language/style/understandability, mutual discussion to identify less useful or redundant items, and then a pretest/pilot test to evaluate internal consistency and eliminate poor items. The latter is particularly important for the specific purposes of Tay (2020c), which was to conduct a factor analysis of responses (discussed in great detail in the next section). Table 2 shows the final product of fifteen survey items equally distributed among the five functions.

The example given in Table 2 is just one illustration of how linguists and therapists, and, by extension, professionals in other domains, can collaborate in a deeper way. It is important to see that the key underlying principles and initiatives taken by the linguist: (i) formulate a clear, stepwise collaborative plan that includes as much discussion as possible, (ii) do not assume a monopoly on metaphor knowledge and always check if it 'makes sense' in the professional context, and relatedly, (iii) recognize the limits of linguistically informed perspectives on therapy even though the latter is supposed to be 'language-constituted.'

2.2 Deploying Therapists as Confederates

Confederates are actors in an experiment. They behave in systematically predetermined ways to elicit responses from genuine naïve participants who are the real subjects of interest and usually unaware of their confederate status.

Table 1 Collaboratively constructed metaphorical versus literal vignettes

Metaphorical vignette	Literal vignette
T: 这学期的学习怎么样? So how is your schoolwork going this semester? C: 不怎么样。 Not too well. T: 能多讲讲吗? Can you tell me more? C: 嗯, 这学期的课程都很难, 就觉得什么都很难, 就觉得好像, 我已经很努力了, 但是感觉还是有很强的力量把我往下拉似的, 就把所有的事情都变得更难。Well, courses are pretty hard. It just feels like everything is difficult, like I have been trying my best but it feels like there's this huge force that's pulling me down and making everything harder. I've been hiking since I was young but this mountain is just too difficult for me. Do you see what I mean? T: 这学期感觉特别漫长特别艰难, 是不是? It's been a long and difficult semester, hasn't it? C: 对。 Yes. T: 能不能告诉我为什么这座山这么难爬。Tell me why this climb this mountain has been particularly difficult. C: 就是太费精力, 太费劲了。特别多的事情要做。要是说我中间停一下, 歇一下也还好, 但是就感觉好像刚读完这本书然后再后天又要交一份作业, 然后就觉得都没有能停下来的时候, 你就只是一直往上爬呀爬呀, 但是感觉永远看不到终点。It takes so much energy and effort. There's so much work to do. It might be okay if I get to stop and rest for a bit,	T: 这学期的学习怎么样? So how is your schoolwork going this semester? C: 不怎么样。 Not too well. T: 能多讲讲吗? Can you tell me more? C: 嗯, 这学期的课程都很难, 就觉得什么都很难, 就觉得好像, 我已经很努力了, 但是感觉还是有很强的力量把我往下拉似的, 就把所有的事情都变得更难。Well, courses are pretty hard. It just feels like everything is difficult, like I have been trying my best but it feels like there's this huge force that's pulling me down and making everything harder. Do you see what I mean? T: 这学期感觉特别漫长特别艰难, 是不是? It's been a long and difficult semester, hasn't it? C: 对。 Yes. T: 能不能告诉我为什么这学期这么难 Tell me why this semester has been particularly difficult. C: 就是太费精力, 太费劲了。特别多的东西要做。要是说我中间停一下, 歇一下也还好, 但是就感觉好像刚读完这本书然后再后天又要做报告。就觉得都没有能停下来的时候, 你就只是一直拼命地做这个做那个, 但是感觉好像永远没个完。It takes so much energy and effort. There's so much work to do. It might be okay if I get to stop and

but I just finished this book and there's an assignment due the next day, and then a presentation due the next day. There's no stopping and all you do is keep climbing higher and higher, but I can never see where it'll ends!

T: 那你在爬这座山的时候，什么感觉呢? So how have you been feeling as you climb this mountain of work?

C: 就特别抑郁，特别不开心。真的很不开心。尤其是我看别人，就像大家都在爬这座山嘛，但是别人感觉都很开心，往上走得特别轻松，但是我觉得像一步一步特别痛苦地往上爬似的。对他们来说好像周末出去玩像爬个山似的，看着路上的风景什么的很开心，到我这儿就不是这样子。让我感觉自己不够厉害，就一直问自己说怎么自己这么挫。Very depressed and upset. It's really hard to tell you how screwed up this is. Especially when I look at others, I feel that we're all these people on this hiking trip, but others are having fun and moving up so easily, but here I am taking these very painful steps. To them it's almost like a relaxing weekend hike and they're enjoying the scenery and all that, but not me. And it makes me feel I'm not good enough and I keep asking myself, why am I so weak?

T: 听起来你是经历了很焦虑的状态啊。像你说的，因为这条路特别陡爬得特别费劲，你都没办法去关注那些美好的事物，比

rest for a bit, but I just finished this book and there's an assignment due the next day, and then a presentation the next day. There's no stopping and all you do is keep working harder and harder, and it feels like it'll never be over!

T: 那你在忙这学期学业这个过程中，什么感觉呢? So how have you been feeling as you handle this semester of work?

C: 就你很难跟你讲这个有多不爽。真的很抑郁，特别不开心。尤其是我看别人，就感觉大家其实都上一样的课嘛，但是别人就很开心，然后学得也特别轻松，但是到我这儿就觉得特别困难。对他们来说这学期感觉轻松，而且他们也挺享受整个过程的，但我这就不是这样的。让我感觉自己不够厉害，就一直问自己说怎么自己这么挫。Very depressed and upset. It's really hard to tell you how screwed up this is. Especially when I look at others, I feel that we're all these people taking the same courses, but others are having fun and learning stuff so easily, but here I am finding it so difficult. To them it's almost like a relaxing semester and they're enjoying the process and all that, but not me. And it makes me feel I'm not good enough and I keep asking myself, why am I so weak?

T: 听起来你是经历了很焦虑的状态啊。像你说的，因为这学期特别困难，特别费劲，你都没办法去关注那些美好的事物，比如

Table 1 (cont.)

Metaphorical vignette	Literal vignette
如路上的风景啊，一起爬山的朋友们的陪伴啊什么的。Sounds like you've been experiencing a lot of anxiety. Like you said, because the path has been so steep and drained so much of your energy, you haven't been able to focus on the pleasurable things like the scenery, the company of your fellow travelers, and all that. C: 可能吧。但是我不知道怎么去关注这些东西啊。Maybe, but I don't know how. T: 我们一直在讲，说你在这个爬这个上坡路时候的感受。其实我不知道你有没有想过用另外一种方式去看它，就是你去想象你的学业这些其实是一个艺术作品，比如一个雕塑或者一个手工艺品什么的。你不是要和别人比赛看谁先跑到那个终点，而是用你的精力去关注你这个最终做的作品，它是很独特的，只属于你一个人的，一个能让你自己感到骄傲的成品。它不会说比别人的更好或者更差。We've been talking about how you feel on this exhausting uphill climb. I wonder if you've actually thought about it in another way, that is to imagine your studies as a unique artwork, like a statue or handicraft. Not trying to race others to the same destination, but focusing your energy on an end product that is uniquely yours, that you can be proud of. Not better or worse than others.	你学到的有用的知识啊，一起上课的这些朋友们的陪伴啊什么的。Sounds like you've been experiencing a lot of anxiety. Like you said, because this semester has been so difficult and drained so much of your energy, you haven't been able to focus on the pleasurable things like the useful knowledge you're learning, the company of your classmates, and all that. 我们一直在讲，说你在这么难的一个学期里的感受。其实我不知道你有没有想过用另外一种方式去看它，就是去想象你的学业最后的结果是只属于你一个人的。不用想着和别人比，而是用你的精力去关注你这个最终的结果，它是很独特的，只属于你一个人的，一个能让你自己感到骄傲的结果。它不会说比别人的更好或者更差。We've been talking about how you feel during this exhausting semester. I wonder if you've actually thought about it in another way, that is to understand that your studies result in something that is uniquely yours. Not trying to compare with others, but focusing your energy on an outcome that is uniquely yours, that you can be proud of. Not better or worse than others.

Table 2 Collaboratively constructed survey items

Function	Item
Build collaborative relationship	1. The therapist and client can work effectively together 2. The therapist is able to see things from the client's point of view 3. The client feels understood by the therapist
Express emotions and experiences	4. The client effectively expresses how he/she feels about his studies to the therapist 5. The client effectively describes his/her experiences to the therapist 6. The therapist and client are able to express abstract things in concrete ways
Explain difficult concepts	7. The therapist is able to summarize and explain the client's situation 8. The therapist is able to explain difficult concepts to the client 9. The client can understand the therapist's advice
Introduce new frames of reference	10. The therapist is able to help the client change their perspective 11. The therapist is able to suggest new ways of looking at the problem 12. The therapist has offered the client a possible solution to their problems
Work through client resistance	13. The client's problems can be comfortably discussed with the therapist 14. The client is willing to open up and share their thoughts with the therapist 15. The therapist makes the suggestions easy for the client to accept

Their use is often inevitable in many social-psychological studies because the target behaviors and responses are not likely to occur with sufficient systematicity or regularity otherwise. However, their deployment in language-related research is more controversial. They are fairly common in developmental pragmatics and language acquisition studies because subjects of interest, such as infants and novice language learners, need them (Long, 1983; Matthews et al., 2010). Ethnographic approaches like conversation analysis, however, emphasize the sequential organization of social interaction in 'genuine' everyday settings (Heritage, 1984; Levinson, 1983), thus the use of confederates is inappropriate by definition. Besides these theoretical concerns, there are also potential ethical issues, such as deception or stereotyping, when confederates' actions may mislead, or reinforce preconceptions about social norms of certain groups of people (Gino et al., 2009).

The aforementioned debate is directly relevant to the study of psychotherapy language and interaction. On the one hand, there is little doubt that ethnographic approaches can shed light on the underlying mechanisms of therapeutic processes with minimal risk to authenticity and ethicality (Antaki et al., 2005; Peräkylä et al., 2011). On the other hand, secondary analyses of uncontrolled data might have limited clinical impact in the long run. They may uncover interesting hypotheses but do not allow us to directly compare different linguistic techniques, interventions, and their outcomes in ways analogous to randomized controlled trials expected in many psychotherapy contexts (Nathan, 1996). Linguists who subscribe to this view need to formulate clear guidelines and procedures with collaborating therapists who are necessarily the ones performing the confederate role. These guidelines should facilitate the linguistic conditions being tested while minimizing their possible impact on co-occurring therapeutic processes in which they are embedded. They should also be clearly spelled out in publications, grant proposals, etc., as good methodological practice. As mentioned in the preceding section, funding bodies and ethical review boards expect a transparent account of the roles and responsibilities of all collaborators, including confederates and the potential risks involved. These are discussed in more detail in Bos (2020) and Israel (2015).

Alongside an excellent overview of major issues and examples, Kuhlen and Brennan (2013) recommend how to maximize the pros and minimize the cons of confederates in linguistic interaction research. Many of these recommendations are broadly applicable to the context of psychotherapy (Tay, 2020a), with adaptions where necessary for the objectives at hand. To illustrate this broad application, Figure 1 is a highly schematic design of a typical experimental trial involving a therapist confederate, also discussed in more detail in Section 4. It begins with an initial timed interaction period that aims to be highly standardized across conditions. Besides a common topic, the confederate should minimize obviously different interactional behavior (e.g., gestures and vocal features)

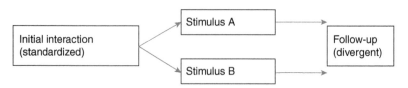

Figure 1 A schematic experimental trial design

with different people, and trials involving stimulus A versus B (e.g., a metaphor versus nonmetaphor) could be arranged intermittently to reduce learning effects. After this, the different stimuli are presented as embedded in the ongoing interaction. A spontaneous follow-up period is then observed as divergent outcomes of the different conditions.

The first recommendation is to ensure that scripted utterances constituting the stimuli occur as infrequently as possible. In our example, the delivery of a scripted metaphorical versus nonmetaphorical prompt occurs only once after the initial interaction. The target of observation unfolds thereafter as spontaneous follow-up interaction to these prompts, largely preserving the authenticity of therapeutic processes. The confederate may require careful co-ordination from the linguist (or another assistant) in terms of things like timing the length of the initial interaction. Next, the linguist should ensure and emphasize that the need for the confederate is based on the need for their professional skills to enhance the validity of interaction rather than convenience. It is not uncommon for a primarily linguistic study to aim at 'implications for practice' and do away with actual therapists and clients to avoid the confederate issue altogether. When the decision is made to use confederates, the design should therefore aim to tap upon their skills as much as possible by minimizing its nonauthentic moments. The linguist should also ensure that the therapist confederate has task initiative as producer rather than addressee of the stimuli. This allows better control over each experimental trial and, more importantly, ensures that clients' expectations toward the confederate as their therapist are not undermined in any way by the design. In other words, from the client's perspective, the scripted stimuli are likely to be experienced as typical rather than atypical of the therapist. Lastly, even though the confederate has task initiative at the critical juncture, the rest of the experimental trial should be as collaborative as possible, since participants are more likely to behave authentically if they believe that they are working together on a genuine goal. It turns out that collaborative coconstruction is widely regarded as an ideal in psychotherapy interaction (Mathieson et al., 2015a), which should be highlighted more explicitly as a point of justification for the use of confederates.

2.3 Toward 'Correspondent Analysis' with Therapists

As mentioned in Section 2.1, it is natural for therapists interested in metaphors to pay more attention to their actual clinical use than to theoretical constructs like domains and mappings. This partly explains the proliferation and interchangeable usage of many different therapeutic definitions of metaphor, some of which in fact include other tropes like metonymy (McMullen, 2008). It also implies that metaphor identification and analysis ought to be closely tied to 'what is going on' at the (co)textual site of a metaphor's occurrence. In more structural-functional approaches to metaphor, there has been an increasing emphasis on attaining analytical consistency by calibrating metaphor identification and coding schemes, and quantifying the resulting agreement among a group of analysts (Pragglejaz Group, 2007; Steen et al., 2010). In a cross-disciplinary collaborative context, however, a complementary strategy is to highlight the diversity of analytical perspectives in a systematic, transparent, and replicable way. Psychotherapy provides excellent grounds for demonstrating such a strategy, especially when analyzing rich exchanges of metaphors by therapists and clients in spontaneous interaction. This is because when the two different analytical perspectives – therapeutic and linguistic – are applied to the same dataset, they can often quite literally be 'superimposed' on each other to identify areas for further collaborative analysis and theorization. The logic and procedures of such 'correspondent analysis' can be stated in fairly general terms. It essentially involves (i) the therapist identifying and annotating transcript portions that reflect important therapeutic processes, (ii) the linguist doing the same for phenomena of interest, such as metaphors in this case, and (iii) intersecting the two to identify overlaps and/or juxtapositions that could lead to further insight. I will now discuss two specific examples applying this strategy (cf. Tay, 2016c; Tay & Neimeyer, 2021). They show how therapists' attention to both the content and structure of unfolding therapy talk can be insightful.

The first example is from a collaborative analysis of fifteen hours of talk from a single therapist–client dyad. As with many other cases of qualitative metaphor research, findings of interest were expected to emerge from a close contextual reading of the data, rather than being anticipated beforehand. The linguist opted for the discourse dynamics approach to identify metaphor vehicle terms (Cameron & Maslen, 2010) as it better reflects the nature of metaphorical conceptualizations in therapy talk. On his part, the therapist quickly observed that the client was exhibiting transferential behavior throughout the session. This refers to the tendency to project past relationships and experiences onto present ones as a result of unresolved feelings, attitudes, and behaviors (Grant & Crawley, 2002). The following (translated) exchange was marked by the therapist to be particularly indicative. The italicized expressions are metaphor vehicle terms independently identified by the linguist prior to the therapist's observations. The expressions in bold were subsequently identified only after intersecting the two sets of observations at step (iii) – that is, the co-occurrence/proximity of metaphors and transferential behavior. This example illustrates how systematic collaborative analysis results in insights that would be missed otherwise. The client was facing severe conflicts with her son and ex-husband. She was frustrated at not being able to 'save' her son who had his own psychological issues, and angry at her ex-husband for apparently not trying hard enough to help.

1. T: 恩。一谈起爸爸这部分啊, 你的感觉是? Right, how do you feel when your father is mentioned?
2. C: 很开心。Very happy.
3. T: 很开心! 恩, 马上来了啊。立刻感觉很开心! 恩。还有呢? Very happy! Right, the *happiness comes immediately*! Right, what else?
4. C: 很温馨啊。Very *warm*.
5. T: 哦。这个好父亲的很棒的父亲的一个形象啊。Oh, that's an *image* of a good father.
6. C: 对。Yes.
7. T: 恩, 很温馨。能说的具体一点吗? Right, very *warm*. Can you be more *concrete*?
8. C: 他什么事情总是站在你的角度去想问题。他总是去呵护你。He always considers things *from your perspective*. He always protects you. (several intermittent turns)
9. C: 那时候我不能理解这些东西。但是一下岗以后, 我才觉得我父亲讲的很多话是对的。因为人是没有危机感的时候, 他不会感觉到那些东西。那我现在也是希望 (儿子名字) 能感觉这种危机感。**Back then** I couldn't understand these things. But after I was laid off, I realized that my father was right in many ways, because someone who does not have a sense of crisis will not sense these things. **Now** I wish (son's name) could also have this sense of crisis.
10. T: 。。。这跟父亲的那句话有关系吗? 就是我, 就我做事还是比较抓紧时间的啊'。... When you said that you like to "*seize the moment*" when you handle things, does it have anything to do with what your father used to do?
11. C: 对。Yes. (several intermittent turns)
12. C: 但是我爸爸的缺点就是一个, 那就是, 那我爸没有把, 至少是你把自己工作搞好, 他再没有把家搞好, 没有把小孩搞好, 那我觉得作为一个男人是失败的。But my father had a flaw, that is, even if he managed his work well, **he did not** manage his family and children well. That, I think, is a failure for a man.
13. T: 作为一个男人有一部分是失败的。As a man, he failed in part.
14. C: 恩对呀。我觉得你只顾你自己, 对吧? 你没有去管老婆, 也不能怪我妈抱怨一辈子, 对吧。你没把小孩搞好。那从我现在看来, 那我觉得在儿子我们也有很多不对的地方。那我就想怎么去引导儿子，去把他搞好。Yes. I think you only care for yourself, right? **You did not** care for your wife. You cannot blame my mother for complaining all her life, right? **You did not** manage your children well. So *from my present perspective*, I feel that there are also many things we are doing wrong for our son. So I am thinking of how to *guide* my son, to manage him well.

A 'pure' linguistic/discursive analysis that focuses on metaphor vehicle terms might proceed as follows. There are a fair number of conventional metaphorical expressions such as "warm," "comes," "image," "from your/my perspective," and "guide" used by both therapist and client, but none of them appear to be elaborated or coconstructed in theoretically striking ways. Line 7 is interesting in that the therapist invites the client to be more "concrete," which implies that the "warm" metaphor is somehow inadequate to express her positive feelings even though such expressions are supposed to help concretize abstract things.

However, once this extract is considered in light of the therapist's observation of transferential behavior, the linguist's attention to metaphor is necessarily broadened to how the client's past *as a whole* becomes a source of metaphorical projection to the present. The invitation to be more 'concrete' can now be interpreted not as a request for local elaboration of "warm," but as an elaboration of the client's past experiences with her father as a whole. This is again observed in Line 10 as the therapist gradually tries to make the client aware that her relationship with her son could in many ways be subconsciously shaped by her relationship with her father. The specific metaphor vehicle terms previously identified by the linguist thus become more like 'satellite metaphors' built around the underpinning, but linguistically uninstantiated high-level metaphor PRESENT IS PAST. With this new insight, the linguist further identifies the bold expressions as indications of a 'past-present' utterance structure (e.g., "back then ... now," "you did not ... from my present perspective") that support the gradual elaboration of the PRESENT IS PAST 'transferential metaphor.' The eventual outcome of this correspondent analysis is an account of how the psychological dynamics of transference are discursively constructed and 'worked through,' with metaphors playing a central role.

Our next example illustrates correspondent analysis at a more structural rather than substantive level of sources and targets. It is easy for linguists focusing on different units of metaphor in therapy to overlook the fact that they are embedded within an (ideally) developing therapeutic process, be it across sessions or within a single session (cf. Tay 2020d, Tay and Qiu 2022).

Even if the linguist has the explicit objective of tracking metaphors across, say, a single session, the operationalization of 'sessional progress' might be done in intuitive or theoretically familiar ways, such as equally timed segments, number of conversational turns, or some other discourse/conversation analytic construct (Tay, 2017a). From a therapist's perspective, however, such measures might not validly reflect unfolding therapeutic processes as observed or planned through the lenses of particular psychotherapy approaches. Although it would be fine for the linguist to pursue a purely discourse analytic objective and rely on the aforementioned constructs as a point of departure, this would represent a missed opportunity to investigate overlaps and juxtapositions between the two.

Consider the specific example of a popular approach known as 'grief therapy.' Grief therapists aim to help clients cope with the loss of loved ones, especially when their deaths are sudden, horrific, or in other ways that challenge their sense of identity, security, and personal narratives about how life should be (Currier et al., 2006). We may expect many metaphors in the process of guiding clients through 'meaning reconstruction' where events surrounding the death and its implications for clients' lives are retold, and relationships with the deceased are re-experienced and redefined through memories, images, etc. (Goldberg & Stephenson, 2016; Nadeau, 2006). An important detail that is easily overlooked, however, is that this process requires careful management of at least two different forms of 'narrative activity' (Neimeyer & Thompson, 2014): the need to process the event story of the death itself, and to access the backstory of the relationship to the deceased. The first of these is critical in helping clients make sense of the traumatic death event that might have threatened their basic sense of meaning in life, and the second gives clients an opportunity to resolve 'unfinished business' and restore some attachment security with the deceased. This implies an expectant structure underlying the use of metaphors, and the session(s) in general, that might play out from simple and conventional to highly complex and creative ways (Hooghe et al., 2012). Even in its simplest form, where the narrative activities unfold linearly with sessional progress, therapists' input would be crucial in identifying the boundaries where different (sub)activities/segments occur, after which linguists may explicitly consider how they interact with metaphor use. Figure 2 is a basic diagram comparing two analytic logics without (left) and with correspondent analysis (right).

On the left is an example of identifying and analyzing metaphor-related constructs and/or phenomena without explicit consideration of how the target session progresses from a therapist's perspective. The consequence is that how constructs x and y are related to, or distributed across, motivated sessional

Therapeutic progress	Metaphor construct #1	Metaphor construct #2	Therapeutic progress	Metaphor construct #1	Metaphor construct #2
	$X_1, X_2, X_3... X_n$	$Y_1, Y_2, Y_3... Y_n$	Segment 1	X_1	Y_1
			Segment 2	X_2	Y_2
			Segment 3	X_3	Y_3
			Segment 4	X_4	Y_4

Figure 2 Basic analytic logic without and with correspondent analysis

segments cannot be modeled effectively. The right-hand side illustrates one particular application of correspondent analysis, wherein the therapist provides crucial input by identifying and annotating transcript portions that reflect important therapeutic processes. The linguist does the same for metaphors, and the resulting alignment between metaphors and segments affords an opportunity for both substantive and structural analysis of metaphor use. A recent example that applies this approach to a single session of grief therapy is Tay and Neimeyer (2021). The second author, an experienced practitioner and researcher, discerned eighteen therapeutically meaningful segments from a single session with a client who was struggling with marital issues as well as prolonged grief over her mother's death. It is important to reiterate the difference between simply segmenting the session into eighteen equal parts, and identifying meaningful transitions, boundaries, etc. The former might be performed for the sake of analytic convenience and/or by the linguist on account of basic methodological considerations alone (Tay, 2017a). The latter, on the other hand, is ideally based on the therapist's personal reflection on the unfolding therapeutic processes, and thus has the advantage of greater external validity. After this segmentation, the frequencies of various metaphorical sources at both image-schematic and idiosyncratic levels (cf. Kimmel, 2012; Tay, 2013) were derived per segment. This gave rise to two distinct analytic possibilities: basic time series analyses to track which types of sources were more common during which phases (cf. Tay 2017c), and correlational analyses between sources to examine how they tend to couple/diverge across the eighteen phases. For example, it was found that the normalized frequencies of image-schematic sources SPACE, OBJECT, and FORCE were strongly mutually correlated across the eighteen therapist-defined phases. This was interpreted as providing an enduring inferential logic whereby dealing with the clients' emotional states is construed as a forceful activity requiring a strong sense of agency (FORCE), and dealing with the overall situation is like shifting around (OBJECT) in an imagined physical space (SPACE). Referring back to Figure 2, the three image schemas are the metaphor constructs x, y (and z). Without correspondent analysis, their co-occurrences throughout the motivated phases are not accounted for, and the aforementioned interpretation would be impossible to derive. With correspondent analysis, the eighteen defined phases turned the frequencies at each phase into a meaningful quantity. Tay and Neimeyer (2021) further explicate how such analyses can also pinpoint striking examples in context that can be further elaborated in terms of how they contribute to the objectives of grief therapy.

We will discuss clients in the next section, but, as explained in Section 1, the emphasis will be on dealing with client variability in metaphor responses rather than on client–researcher collaboration. Nevertheless, some of the collaborative approaches just described have the potential to work well with clients. Correspondent analysis – the superimposition of different viewpoints – offers intriguing possibilities for future work, to the extent that client views, feedback, and so on could be systematically couched as a formal analytical perspective.

3 Modeling Variability in Client Responses

One of the most striking claims of CMT is that a large number of conceptual metaphors seem to be universal. Typical examples include LIFE IS A JOURNEY, ANGER IS HEAT, and ARGUMENT IS WAR, all of which have source domains that seem to be grounded in universal bodily experiences. Cultural, contextual, and individual variations are not outrightly denied, but are treated as epiphenomenal to the core of invariant embodied experiences that underpin these 'metaphors we live by' (Grady, 1997; Johnson, 1987; Lakoff & Johnson, 1980, 1999). There is no need to rehearse the many objections from cultural anthropology (Quinn, 1991) to cognitive psychology (Glucksberg & McGlone, 1999) to the sweeping idea that human conceptual systems are reducible to a core set of cross-domain mappings motivated by bodily experiences. Recent theoretical and empirical studies are in fact increasingly regarding metaphor variation as a norm, and are attempting to model the nature and extent of this variation across cultures, contexts, and individuals as directly and explicitly as possible (Kövecses, 2020).

In the psychotherapy context, variability in metaphor use, understanding, and appreciation is a crucial yet seldom-discussed phenomenon. This is partly because a focus on variability could be perceived to be at odds with the premise that metaphors are generally 'effective.' It is not difficult to understand the pragmatism behind the tendency to downplay such variability in a context where a high premium is placed on efficacy and effectiveness associated with 'standard' interventions. At the same time, however, the advocacy of client agency and 'patient-centeredness' (Mead & Bower, 2000) strongly implies that researchers and therapists alike should be prepared to see the illness through the patient's eyes (McWhinney, 1993). The need to do so is confirmed by the fact that client expectations, beliefs, attitudes, etc., toward treatment are demonstrably linked to outcomes (Greenberg et al., 2006). Client responses to metaphors are of particular interest in this regard. Compared to the therapist's perspective of metaphors as a technique or resource that can be learned and applied (Blenkiron, 2010; Stott et al., 2010), how clients perceive or react to metaphors are likely to be far more varied, spontaneous, and observable across different levels and phases of the treatment process. Client responses may also provide important clues to the potential pitfalls of metaphor use in some cases. It is thus important for linguists, who might have fewer opportunities to observe these through first-hand interactions with clients, to be prepared to deal with them both methodologically and analytically. It should be noted that therapists can also have different styles and vary accordingly in their metaphor use and response, and this constitutes an interesting topic in its own right. Besides those explained earlier, another reason for focusing on client rather than therapist variability is pragmatic in nature. From experience, it is far more plausible to examine how different clients seeing the same therapist vary, holding one half of the equation constant and simplifying data collection. The reverse, however, is less likely to be realistic.

The relative lack of opportunities to interact with actual clients raises the practical question of whether role-played or simulated clients could be used instead. Simulations, and related techniques such as scripted vignettes, are in fact not uncommon in (mental) health education and research, with ongoing debate about their value and effectiveness (Kaplonyi et al., 2017; Lane & Rollnick, 2007; Nestel & Tierney, 2007; Riley et al., 2021). For psychotherapy, the case for simulations is often made on the grounds that they circumvent ethical issues like privacy and confidentiality (Matthews et al., 2014), and there is some evidence to suggest that simulated and actual clients do not differ significantly (Finger et al., 1993; Hodgson et al., 2007). This presents an interesting contrast with the case of confederate therapists discussed in the previous section – (partially) 'fake' therapists might be ethically problematic, but fake clients are the opposite. While it is beyond the present scope to discuss this issue in great detail, the general advice is that the merits of simulated clients depend on the specific objectives of the planned study, and need to be explicitly argued for in each case. In the studies to be introduced in this section, for example, the use of simulated clients for interviews, surveys, and even psychophysiological measures can all be argued to be acceptable in the event that actual clients are unavailable.

We begin by outlining how variability in client responses to metaphor can manifest across different forms and levels, from survey to psychophysiological and discourse data. Two aspects of this variability will then be discussed in greater detail: (i) that which is relatively self-apparent from qualitative data like interviews and spontaneous client talk, and (ii) that which is often hidden within the structure of survey, experimental, and other types of quantitative data. In line with the aforementioned trend in contemporary research, it is important to emphasize that the ideal objective in these cases is not to attempt to control for variability, but to present and model it as explicitly as possible.

3.1 Types of Client Response

One might wrongly assume that 'client responses' refer only to how clients react to therapists' use of metaphors during their spontaneous face-to-face interactions. In fact, there are different types of response that can be systematically investigated along the three parameters of context, target, and mode. These are represented in Table 3.

The *context* of response distinguishes spontaneous reactions to metaphor during therapy interaction from more deliberate evaluations outside of treatment. The existing literature has been far more concerned with the former, with little attention to perceptions and attitudes toward metaphor in related nonclinical settings, such as psychoeducation and feedback activities. The *target* of response distinguishes responses to specific metaphors in a particular context (e.g., T: how do you feel as you <u>unload the burden</u>?) from reactions to higher levels of metaphor use, such as a general metaphorical 'style' of communication. Existing literature has likewise tended to focus on the former, as they often more concretely manifested. Lastly, the *mode* of response ranges from (relatively) conscious and deliberate feedback, like utterances and survey responses, to unconscious feedback beyond clients' locus of control, like psychophysiological reactions to metaphor use. We again see a disproportionate focus in the literature on conscious rather than unconscious feedback, overlooking the latter as a critical source of variability in responses to metaphor.

Table 3 Types of client response to metaphor

CONTEXT / TARGET	MODE			
	Conscious		Unconscious	
	Specific	General	Specific	General
During treatment	A	B	C	D
Outside of treatment	E	F	G	H

The cells in Table 3 identify eight specific contexts (A–H) that each generates unique data on client response to metaphor and its variability. We will discuss four of these contexts: (i) conscious reactions to specific metaphors during therapy (A), (ii) semi-structured interviews on general views of metaphor outside therapy (F), (iii) survey ratings of specific metaphors outside therapy (E), and (iv) unconscious skin conductance responses to a metaphorical communication style during therapy (D). This will be organized under two subsections. The first subsection illustrates variability that is relatively self-apparent, in that differences among views of metaphor are directly expressed and observable from qualitative data like talk and interviews. The second subsection focuses on variability that is more subtle and requires some quantitative analytical techniques to uncover. The implications of each type of variability will also be discussed.

3.2 Self-Apparent Variability in Talk and Interview Data

Therapist–client talk usually offers the most direct and grounded insights into how different clients react and respond to metaphors. It is also amenable to the types of structural and/or functional discourse analytic modeling often seen in other discourse contexts. The following three examples are all similar in that the therapist explicitly affirms the use of metaphors and tries to develop their inferential potential with the client, notwithstanding some differences in how this was done. They outline a simple continuum of client attitudes, ranging from an obvious eagerness to expressions of negativity toward metaphor.

1. T: 嗯。我的心灵得到自由， 同时又跟我的这个年龄可有的性的能量，满足和吸引力 交织在一起 Right. My soul is free, and it is woven together with the sexual vitality, satisfaction, and attractiveness I could have at my age.
2. C: 他们好像就是一个源泉，不断的在给我传递着，那种清新，不断的在. …… They are like a fountain, constantly giving me that freshness, constantly …
3. T: 哎, 源泉源泉, 源泉, 这个词好! 是不是那些不好的感觉, 离我们是不是远了? Ah, fountain, fountain, fountain, good description! Is it, those bad feelings, are they far away from us now?
4. C: 都被冲的一干二净了, 他那源泉他会散发出那种很神奇的东西, 能让我那个千疮百孔的具有治疗作用, 让他们慢慢的好好起来, 他会散发出许多诱人的气味, 草长莺 飞, 他会滋润我的内心, 让那些本来那一片火海的东西, 浇灭它 All flushed clean. That fountain radiates something very miraculous, it can repair my damage, let them slowly heal. It radiates many tempting aromas, like a scenic end of spring, it nourishes my heart, it extinguishes what was originally a sea of fire.

In the first example, the client was a victim of childhood sexual abuse by a close relative, resulting in lingering trauma and a lack of sexual confidence in adulthood. The therapist had initiated a visualization exercise wherein the client imagined an ideal alternative situation for himself. While the therapist's initial utterance contains a novel metaphor ("my soul is free . . . woven together") that would have provided a good starting point for metaphorical elaboration, the client produces his own spontaneous novel metaphor of a "fountain." This was affirmed with enthusiasm by the therapist (Line 3) and independently extended in an impressive manner afterward (Line 4). The interaction seems to suggest a high level of client engagement, or willing participation in therapeutic activities, which has been associated with positive treatment outcomes (Holdsworth et al., 2014). It would be useful to model how responses to metaphor co-occur with different measured engagement levels in more concrete structural-functional terms, like the multiple (mixed) sources and targets produced in quick succession within a single turn: "radiate," "repair," "heal," "aromas," "scenic end of spring," "a sea of fire." This brief exchange would be a poster child for theoretical literature that advocates metaphor use in psychotherapy but consequently downplays the type of variability in responses seen in the following examples.

1. C: 可能是做事情什么都太不成熟了。就比如跟小树似的, 还是一棵小幼苗。 但别人可能都是参天大树。但是我就是个小幼苗 Maybe everything I do is quite immature. Like a small tree, or a seedling. Maybe everyone else is a big tree but I am just a seedling.
2. T: 嗯, 你觉得幼苗是什么样子的? 在你看来 Okay. What do you think the seedling is like?
3. C: 幼苗, 在我看来就是跟那些大树比, 总之就是比较脆弱, 在我看来就是 The seedling, I think when compared to those big trees, is more fragile, I think so.
4. T: 那你这个幼苗的周围是什么样子的? So, what are the surroundings like for this seedling?
5. C: 周围有可能会觉得人家都是树, 就我自己是幼苗 Maybe everyone around me is a big tree, and I am the only seedling.
6. T: 都有什么样的树呢, 在你的周围? 周围的环境都是什么样的呢, 如果你来描述的话 What kinds of trees are around you? How would you describe the surroundings?

In our second example, the client was a university student experiencing anxiety over her academic performance and perceived lack of maturity compared to her peers. Similar to the client in the first example, she initiated a novel metaphorical self-description as a "small tree or seedling" and those around her as a "big tree." The therapist likewise invites her to elaborate this metaphor in visual terms (Kopp & Craw, 1998), but does this over three turns (Lines 2, 4, 6) as the client could only offer a relatively limited elaboration each time. Compared to the previous example, it is apparent that this client is equally receptive toward the therapist's focus on metaphor but is less proliferative and requires more prompting. This contrast can again be systematically described in structural-functional terms as having fewer sources and targets over more turns. We now turn to the final example – the kind hardly shown in most therapeutic research on metaphor – where the observably lower level of engagement is likewise reflected by a reluctance and/or inability to respond to metaphor.

1. T: 你也可以把自己想象成这个过程当中的这辆车, 也可以把自己想象成这个人。其实人和车是什么关系呢? 你觉得? You can also imagine yourself as the car or as the owner. What is the relationship between the owner and the car? What do you think?
2. C: 相互依存的Mutually dependent.
3. T: 相互依存的, 但是相处过程种还是会有一些冲突, 主人总归是要依靠他的车的?
   Mutually dependent, but there is still some conflict in the process, the owner ultimately has to rely on his car?
4. C: 嗯Yes.
5. T: 这个车总归也是要依附它主人的This car also has to rely on its owner.
6. C: 嗯Yes.
7. T: 你觉得主人能修复好他和车的这种关系吗? Do you think the owner can fix his relationship with the car?
8. C: 能吧 I guess so.
9. T: 嗯, 是。我们再联想一下自己的实际生活, 有没有遇到类似的这样的一个经历?
   Yes. Let's think about our real life again, have you had a similar experience?
10. C: 现在暂时想不出来。这和我的实际生活有什么关系?
    I can't think of any now. What does this have to do with my real life?

In this example, the therapist uses a photograph of a frustrated man beside his malfunctioning car as a technique to invite the client to talk about his experiences (Ginicola et al., 2012; Stevens & Spears, 2009). The therapist explicitly suggests that the client utilize either the man or the car as a metaphor for himself (Line 1), and by implication the relationship between the two as a metaphor for their current situation. Similar to Example 2, the client's series of responses toward this suggestion appears to be limited (Line 2, 4, 6, 8), prompting the therapist to supply the desired inferences and initiate further elaboration (Line 3, 5, 7). Different than the first two examples, however, the therapist goes one step further to explicitly suggest the intended target topic of this exercise – the client's "real life" (Line 9). While some researchers do encourage therapists to invite clients to map an imagined metaphorical scenario back onto their real life (Kopp & Craw, 1998; Sims, 2003), the client's limited participation may render such a move ineffective or premature. This is seen in the client's subtle show of resistance in Line 10, where he questions the relevance of the picture to his real-life situation. Consistent with the previous examples, there seems to be some relationship between the clients' willingness to work with metaphor and the extent to which they are engaged with the therapy. In general, the circumstances and ways in which clients reject or 'resist' metaphor are still underresearched, but remain important for critical reflection on its presumed utility. They exemplify the broader theoretical notion of 'resistance to metaphor' that has gained recent traction, which concerns how and why people explicitly object to various metaphors in contexts ranging from politics to science and health (Gibbs & Siman, 2021; Wackers et al., 2021). Common reasons like metaphors being seen as meaningless, unscientific, or even offensive are likely to also apply in psychotherapy, and could be investigated in more detail. Furthermore, clear contrasts like Examples 1 and 3 also throw up other relevant questions, such as individual differences in clients' capacities for metaphor use.

Besides spontaneous therapy talk, surveys and interview data can also directly reveal variability in how clients perceive metaphor use. This represents a move from examining responses during treatment to outside of treatment, from responses to specific metaphors like the examples given earlier to the use of metaphor in general, and from spontaneous response to conscious, deliberate reflection in more controlled settings (Table 3). We refer back to the constructed metaphorical versus literal vignettes in Table 1. In addition to the survey study mentioned earlier, participants were also invited to follow-up interviews to reflect and elaborate on their reasons for preferring either vignette. Recall that the vignettes were constructed, in collaboration with a practicing therapist, to showcase five key therapeutic functions that have been claimed to be better performed by metaphorical than literal language: (i) building a collaborative relationship, (ii) expressing emotions and experiences, (iii) explaining difficult concepts, (iv) introducing new frames of reference, and (v) working through client resistance. An important feature of the survey and interviews is their within-subjects design, which means that each participant had to reflect on both metaphorical and literal strategies for performing these functions. This should lead to a more balanced and considered set of reasons for their preferences, which in turn allows us to model variability by inductively categorizing, comparing, and contrasting them.

Table 4 illustrates a sample of reasons for client preferences. Two general aspects were identified from the interview: 'function in context,' which concerns why metaphorical/literal language was thought to be better at performing the functions as the dialogue unfolded, and 'general impression,' which includes comments about metaphorical/literal language in general.

We see some interesting reasons offered by layperson clients that are sometimes discussed by metaphor researchers but seldom in the therapy literature. These include the (overly) 'feminine' quality of metaphors (Zeng et al., 2020) and their potential role in topic management (Angus & Korman, 2002). Nevertheless, the more relevant point here is that the cross-tabulation is useful for uncovering interesting aspects of variability in client responses, especially if we find somewhat similar reasons in different rows within the same column. This would imply that a particular strategy could be perceived as effective or ineffective for the same reasons by different people, and that the 'effectiveness' of metaphors is thus not tied to its inherent characteristics, as is often asserted. The conflicting views on topic management is a case in point, with some saying that metaphors are facilitative and others suggesting that they cause speakers to lose sight of the 'real' topic. There is a need to investigate these differences and

Table 4 Sample client preferences for metaphor versus literal language

Preference / Aspect	Function in context	General impression
Metaphor	• Metaphors create a deeper impression and helps the client remember the discussion • Metaphors result in better flow and topic management • Metaphors are familiar to the client and allows him to take the lead	• Metaphors are more skilful • Metaphors are more logical • Metaphors are more 'friendly'
Literal	• Literal language is more efficient by not beating about the bush • Literal language is more direct and does not lose sight of the real topic • Literal language is more concrete for talking about academic issues	• Metaphors are too literary • Metaphors are too 'chicken soup for the soul' • Metaphors are too feminine

contradictions across client populations, as they play an important role in developing a more critical understanding of when, how, and if metaphors should be used in psychotherapy.

3.3 Subtle Variability in Experimental and Survey Data

Variability in client responses to metaphor can be depicted in terms of both its nature and extent. While qualitative data, such as session transcripts and interviews, can directly reflect and thus help us model the nature of variability, quantitative approaches are helpful for understanding how much variability there is and where it lies. These aspects are usually not apparent from surface observation and need to be uncovered by techniques that deal with the quantitative structure of metaphor-relevant measures across multiple subjects.

We first illustrate this with results from recent experimental studies of skin conductance responses to metaphor during psychotherapy and related activities (Tay, 2020a; Tay et al., 2019). Skin conductance refers to the ability of the skin to conduct electricity, which is measured by applying a constant voltage between two skin contact points and monitoring the resulting current flow between them (Braithwaite et al., 2015). Skin conductance momentarily increases when subjects experience physiological arousal and increased sweat gland activity. Among other inferential possibilities, it could indicate how affectively engaging various types of stimuli are, ranging from different media forms (Potter & Bolls, 2012) to interactional strategies (Stevanovic et al., 2021). 'Affective engagement' is understood here as the degree of emotional and cognitive response toward stimuli, which is related to the much-discussed therapeutic alliance (Horvath & Greenberg, 1994) between counselor and client. Engaged clients are more likely to bond with their counselors, endorse treatment goals, participate more deeply and longer, and report greater satisfaction with their treatment (Thompson et al., 2007). Positive correlations between skin conductance levels and psychotherapeutically relevant measures such as the quality of client experiences (Glucksman et al., 1985), social-emotional interaction (Marci et al., 2007), and perceived counselor empathy (Robinson et al., 1982), have also been reported. In the present research, participants were randomly assigned to either a metaphorical or a literal condition (N=30 each), and their skin conductance levels over an extended period of interaction with the therapist were compared. The metaphorical condition had the therapist introduce an overarching metaphor and probe its inferences for the topic with the client in a spontaneous manner. The topic was 'problems and challenges you might be facing in your studies,' and the metaphor was initiated by a stimulus prompt *can you fully eat through the class* – 'eat through' being a metaphor for 'understand' in Mandarin Chinese. In the literal condition, the same target topic was discussed without explicit appeal to any overarching metaphor. The stimulus prompt was replaced with the literal expression *can you fully understand the class*. Two time intervals were of specific interest: Period 1 (five minutes), which was from the start of the interaction to the stimulus prompt, and Period 3 (five minutes), which was from the start of the client's response to the prompt to the end of the interaction. The intervening Period 2 took place between the end of the stimulus prompt and the start of client's response.

Reflecting the general assumption that metaphors are 'effective' that we have been critically interrogating, the aforementioned design can be seen as a typical setup to investigate the hypothesis that the metaphorical condition is more affectively engaging (Citron & Goldberg, 2014; Levin, 1980) – as evidenced by higher skin conductance levels as the interaction unfolds from Period 1 to 3. Many studies with a comparable design would choose the linear model as the standard approach to statistical analysis of the data. More specifically, this would involve a two-way repeated measures ANOVA with the following (in) dependent variables:

- **Average SCL (skin conductance level).** The dependent variable. This is the average value of continuous skin conductance measurements over Period 1 and Period 3, where a measurement is taken every 0.025s. SCL is measured in µS, the standard unit for conductance
- **Period.** The within-subjects independent variable. The average SCL for Period 1 (before stimulus) would be compared with Period 3 (after stimulus), like a typical 'pre-post' comparison
- **Condition.** The between-subjects independent variable. Average SCLs for Periods 1 and 3 would be compared between subjects in the metaphorical and literal condition

Since the magnitude of 'raw' SCL values can vary greatly between individuals, a range correction formula $SCL_{corrected} = (SCL_{observed} - SCL_{min})/(SCL_{max} - SCL_{min})$ can be used to convert each measurement into a proportion of that individual's SCL range. The average SCL thus ends up as a normalized value between 0 and 1 (Dawson et al., 2007). While this represents a way to control for variability between people, such 'universal' variability in SCL is not inherently related to metaphor response. Our concern lies instead with how (change in) responses across time may vary from person to person, in unexpected ways that cannot be captured by the linear modeling approach described earlier.

Staying with the linear model for now, Figure 3 shows the results of the two-way ANOVA analysis. The bar plots with 95% confidence intervals represent average SCL in Period 1 and 3 across the two conditions, and the superimposed strip plots show the distribution of individual data points. The increase from Phase 1 to 3 is statistically significant ($F(1,58)=37.14$, $p<.001$, $\eta^2_p=0.39$) in both the metaphorical ($t(29)=-6.02$, $p<.001$) and literal ($t(29)=-2.56$, $p=.016$) conditions, suggesting that clients' affective engagement gradually increases with time regardless of metaphor use. However, the interaction between Period and Condition is also significant ($F(1,58)=6.34$, $p=.015$, $\eta^2_p=0.098$), further suggesting that this increase was greater in the metaphorical condition.

This standard analysis appears to support our hypothesis that metaphors are more affectively engaging than literal language across an extended period of interaction. However, it is worth noting that the linear model makes certain assumptions about the data that do not always reflect behavioral realities on the ground in this type of study. The first assumption is that all observations are independent, which requires that (i) the literal and metaphorical conditions AND (ii) each client's SCL values in Periods 1 and 3 do not influence each other. Point (i) is generally unproblematic because the conditions are tested apart from each other. Point (ii) is more problematic because there is reason to believe that each client's SCL values across time are correlated. That is to say, a client's response and hence SCL in Period 3 is likely to be shaped by Period 1, such that within-subject differences are 'clustered,' or closer than between-subject differences. Any realistic estimate of the general differences between

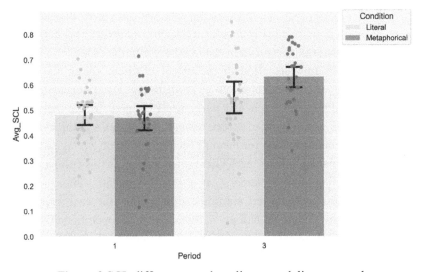

Figure 3 SCL differences under a linear modeling approach

Periods 1 and 3 should therefore take this clustering into account. Relatedly, the linear model uses sample means to produce a single 'fixed' estimate of the expected differences between conditions and time periods. In statistical parlance, we say that the independent variables (Period and Condition) are treated as 'fixed effects,' and the dependent variable (Average SCL) is modeled as the sum of a fixed intercept (i.e., the estimated SCL when the effect of the independent variables is zero) and fixed slopes (i.e., how much the outcome changes when each independent variable changes). It turns out that this standard mathematical formulation obscures the type of client-to-client variability we are discussing. Since we only 'allow' one aggregated difference profile between conditions and periods, the following potential scenarios are not accounted for: (i) idiosyncratic response patterns from Period 1 to 3 that could vary substantially between clients, and (ii) unequal starting/ending points of Period 1 and 3 as some clients think longer after the stimulus and/or inadvertently talk beyond the determined endpoint. Any of these would indicate an 'imbalance' in the design that needs to be handled by more flexible modeling techniques. The superimposed strip plots give us a visual clue that idiosyncratic responses patterns could indeed be present in the data. Average SCLs exhibit greater dispersion (i.e., a higher standard deviation) in the metaphorical condition in Period 1, but this seems to be reversed in Period 3, suggesting that we are unlikely to see a uniform increasing pattern across all subjects.

One such technique that is often used in the social and physical sciences is multilevel or mixed effects modeling (Coupé, 2018; Harrison et al., 2018; Heck & Thomas, 2015). Technical details and instructions for performing it on different computer programs are widely available and will not be repeated here. Two good examples are the detailed user guides that accompany the open–source statistical software jamovi (www.jamovi.org) and JASP (jasp–stats.org). We focus instead on how multilevel modeling provides an explicit representation of the extent of client variability. In a nutshell, mixed effect models allow us to distinguish and consider both fixed and 'random effects,' hence its name. Returning to our potential scenarios, while a purely fixed effects model like ANOVA estimates just one fixed intercept and slope for the influence of Period on average SCL, a random effects model 'allows' each client (the 'cluster,' in this case) to have a different intercept and/or slope. That means the potential idiosyncratic response patterns and uneven starting/ending points for each client is acknowledged by the model and given a mathematical operationalization. Arguably the most elegant feature of multilevel models is that instead of estimating a unique intercept/slope for *every* client, which would undermine statistical power because sample sizes underlying the estimates are greatly reduced, each client's intercept/slope is estimated as a random draw from an underlying normal distribution using just one set of parameters (mean and standard deviation). This also implies that, unlike the ANOVA approach, random effects models can accommodate missing data points due to unforeseen circumstances, such as participants dropping out.

All this is not to say that mixed effect models are always necessary or preferable. In situations where the aforementioned scenarios of variability do not occur, the outcomes of the two approaches will not differ much, such that the flexibility of mixed effect models would not justify their increased complexity (Murtaugh, 2007). It is thus advisable to conduct an initial assessment of variability by visualizing the data in appropriate ways. The strip plots in Figure 3 already provided a visual clue. Taking this further, Figure 4 plots average SCL levels from Period 1 to 3 for each of twenty-four randomly chosen

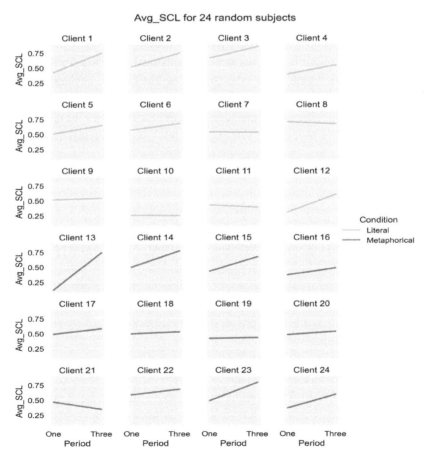

Figure 4 Average SCL across Period 1 and 3 for twenty-four random clients

clients (N=12 for each condition). Literal and metaphorical conditions are indicated by green and red lines respectively.

We can readily observe idiosyncratic response patterns from Period 1 to 3 across the twenty-four clients. Contrary to our general conclusion, a good number of literal condition clients (e.g., 1 to 4) experience a far greater SCL increase than metaphorical condition clients (e.g., 17 to 21). Client 21 in fact experienced a decrease in SCL and would be an interesting candidate, together with clients 1 to 4, for the type of follow-up qualitative interviews discussed in the previous section to gain a deeper understanding of their 'unexpected' attitudes and responses to metaphor. In general, the different slopes exactly reflect the type of individual variability that we want to highlight in our critical consideration of 'one size fits all' claims about metaphor. They also alert us to the fact that mixed effect modelling is most likely going to be appropriate, with each subject's measurements as a cluster.

We therefore fit a mixed effects model with random intercepts for subjects, and Period and Condition remaining as fixed effects. The results of the fixed effects remain unchanged, with a significant interaction effect where SCL increase across periods was greater in the metaphorical condition. To evaluate the random effect, we may refer to two outcomes. The first is a likelihood ratio test (LRT) for random effects, which essentially compares the mixed effects model with a fixed effects-only model in terms of how well it fits the data. The test is significant in this case – $\chi^2(1)=11.22$, $p<.001$ – suggesting that the mixed effects model provides a significantly better fit. The second outcome is the intraclass correlation coefficient (ICC), which indicates the proportion of total variance in the dependent variable that is accounted for by the between-cluster variance (i.e., how much variability there is between subjects): ICC=0.42 (or 42%) in this case, again suggesting that individual variability is a substantial component that should not be overlooked. In summary, we can say for this case that the mixed effect modeling approach is preferable over the fixed effects-only ANOVA approach for providing an explicit account of the presence and extent of idiosyncratic responses to metaphor, without undermining the more general conclusion that metaphors are indeed 'on average' more affectively engaging than literal language.

Our second example of how unexpected responses to metaphor can be buried deep within quantitative data comes from the survey study discussed in the previous section. The focus back then was on therapist input in survey design, but we now consider the actual survey findings from a sample of eighty-four native Mandarin Chinese-speaking university students (forty-six women, *M*=23.5 years, *SD*=3.15). Recall that the survey consisted of fifteen items that capture evaluations of how well five distinct therapeutic functions were performed in the metaphorical versus literal vignette. Each function was represented by three items (Table 2). Since all respondents rated both vignettes in a within-subjects design, a standard linear model of the results would involve comparing average ratings for each function between vignettes using matched pairs t-tests. Let us recall the aforementioned characteristics of the linear model and see how they apply in this case. The independence assumption is less problematic here than in the SCL study since each vignette is independently rated and presented in counterbalanced fashion (i.e., half the respondents read vignette A before B and vice versa) to minimize learning effects. However, sample means are still used to produce single 'fixed' estimates of the differences between vignettes, which might again obscure variability. The results of this analysis did show, as hypothesized, that the metaphorical vignette was rated as more effective in performing all five functions. Rather than fitting another mixed effects model here (e.g., with random intercepts for respondents), we use this example to illustrate another technique to model survey results, known as factor analysis (Reise et al., 2000). The usual purpose of factor analysis when applied to surveys is to discover patterns or groupings not among respondents, but among survey items. Again, technical details and instructions to perform it on different computer programs will not be reproduced here; the aforementioned *jamovi* and JASP are both good options. The central idea of factor analysis is to reduce a large number of variables (i.e., survey items) into a more condensed 'factor structure.' This means smaller groups of items wherein the items within each group are maximally similar to one another, and the groups themselves are maximally dissimilar to one another. Each group is also known as a factor. Similarity is based on how well the item responses are correlated across respondents. A strong correlation between items A and B means that respondents who rated item A high/low also tended to rate item B high/low (or low/high), implying that both items are interpretable as components of a common underlying (theoretical) construct. We say that items A and B are 'loaded' onto the same factor. In the present case, each factor would reflect some broad criterion by which respondents evaluated the metaphorical vignette. On the other hand, if an item is not well correlated with any other items, it would end up as not 'belonging to' or loaded onto any factor. This implies that respondents' views of that item are not aligned with, or predictable from, the rest. Factor analysis is thus useful in two broad and often interrelated ways (Revicki et al., 2014): for confirmatory research to see if the factor structure adequately fits a hypothesized number of factors based on theory, or exploratory research to investigate the factor structure without any theoretical preconceptions. Figure 5 illustrates the fifteen-item factor

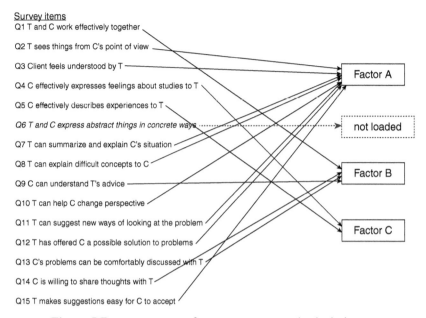

Figure 5 Factor structure of responses to metaphorical vignette

structure of responses to the metaphorical vignette shown in Table 1. Interested readers can refer to Tay (2020c) for details including model fit statistics.

We see that fourteen out of the fifteen items loaded onto three factors. Factor A consists of Q2, 3, 7, 8, 10, 11, 12, and 15, which depict general features of successful communication that could be collectively interpreted as a broad criterion of evaluation. Likewise, Factors B (Q1, 9, 13, 14) and C (Q4, 5) respectively suggest therapist–client collaboration and the expression of emotions and experiences as important criteria for judging the metaphorical vignette. The striking point here is that Q6 (*T and C express abstract things in concrete ways*) ended up as the only unloaded item. It turns out that Q6 is a formulation of one of the most fundamental and accepted properties of metaphor in contemporary research – that which helps to express something abstract in terms of something more concrete (Lakoff, 1993). However, respondents' judgments of how well the metaphor embedded in the vignette achieved this function did not correlate well with their judgments along the other items. This dovetails with the observation that Q6 had the highest standard deviation (SD=1.03) among the fifteen items, and hence the most varied responses. Both findings suggest that respondents were relatively inconsistent, both among themselves and across the fifteen items each one rated, in evaluating whether the metaphor in the vignette did perform the function of helping the therapist and client express abstract things more concretely. This occurred even though the vignette was constructed by the metaphor researcher in consultation with the therapist. Such findings are useful in reminding linguists to always be mindful for gaps between even the most widely embraced theoretical definitions, and the ways in which these definitions are implicitly understood or perceived by language users. More specifically, in the psychotherapy context, they alert both linguists and therapists to the need to guard against an overly optimistic or idealized view about what metaphors are and how they are received by clients. The qualitative examples and quantitative techniques introduced in this section – multilevel modeling and factor analysis – illustrate some methodological avenues to explicitly highlight variable client responses that would otherwise be overlooked if one focuses only on general patterns across entire subject samples.

4 Striking a Balance Between Spontaneity and Control

Psychotherapy has a somewhat paradoxical status as a healthcare practice that seems to comprise almost entirely of 'ordinary' verbal interaction. Casual observers who know it by the nickname 'the talking cure' might be led to believe that therapist–client talk is not too different than a normal conversation between friends (Ferrara, 1994; Mondada, 2010). Some therapists have in fact described themselves as skilled conversationalists or 'master conversational artists,' the main difference being that unlike a chat with friends, they also have the responsibility of managing the therapeutic conversation (Anderson & Goolishian, 1988). The efficacy of psychotherapy would from this perspective depend more on the personal qualities of therapists and subjective judgments of their interactions with clients, both of which often leave behind discourse analytic traces. Unsurprisingly, there are many who criticize such an approach of doing and evaluating therapy as lacking scientific rigor (Association for Psychological Science, 2009). Cognitive behavioral therapy is a good example of a major paradigm that emphasizes the importance of evidence-based practice. This is often understood as the application of 'gold standard' research designs like randomized controlled trials (Dyer & Joseph, 2006) to measure the effects of specific therapeutic interventions under strictly regulated settings (Craske et al., 2014; Sensky et al., 2000; Watts et al., 2013). From this perspective, spontaneous inflections that may arise in the course of therapy – including those of conversation or discourse analytic interest – are often disregarded as trivial epiphenomena that are not part of the tested intervention.

The fundamental tension between these approaches reflects the general perpetual debate between qualitative and quantitative research paradigms. Purton

(2014) reminds us that the stakes are not just methodological in nature, but involve questions like therapists' professional identity and what it means for them to claim to "know what they are doing" (p.1). Linguists of various theoretical persuasions have faced similar issues and devised methodological approaches that, like the ones to be discussed in this section, have proven to be effective in striking the required balance between spontaneity and control for their respective purposes. The 'sociolinguistic interview' technique developed by Labov (1984) is a prime example of eliciting authentic responses across a range of preformulated speech contexts, and continues to inform sociolinguistic research today. Closer to our interest in clinical contexts, conversation analysis is another example where balancing spontaneity and control is in fact argued to be advantageous for traditionally controlled tasks such as assessing aphasia patients' communicative abilities (Boles, 1998; Gerber & Gurland, 1989). Metaphor researchers interested in psychotherapy are likewise faced with a 'customized' set of issues that need to be addressed with appropriate strategies. Consider the following brief exchange with metaphorical expressions italicized.

1. C: I almost don't want to *go down there*. You know, there's *something in me that's released* and I keep on getting ideas about, and instead of *going really down* . . .
2. T: Yeah
3. C: Because . . .
4. T: Yeah. Maybe you ought to *come back up* for a moment and sort of *walk your way back up the steps* for a minute because, and sort of feel *the reversal* too before you *go* completely.
5. C: I don't know. It's like people can feel when there isn't self-concern and they're scared of it, you know? Because I know . . . when *the shit hits the fan*, unless you take care of yourself nobody really is going to. So, if they like find this person whose energy is *getting all gone out there* and they get, you know . . .
6. T: Yeah. Yeah. Like you're *seeing*, you're getting some kind of *clearer* sense of how you seem to other people *in the dark*.
7. C: Yeah. Yeah, I'm really feeling, I'm just getting, I mean I'm only saying one-tenth of the *flashes* I'm getting.

The client initiates two striking metaphors of not wanting to "go down there" to some undesirable metaphorical location, and something inside him that is "released." The therapist likely sensed the potential utility of the first metaphor, spontaneously developing it by encouraging the client to "come back up." In so doing, he overlooks the "release" metaphor which also happens to clash inferentially with the notion of metaphorical movement. In the next two turns, however, this metaphorical movement only gets partially developed as a handful of new metaphors quickly enter the scene. Many discourse analysts looking at this brief interaction would be quick to highlight its spontaneous nature. They might observe that the therapist manages the conversation by selecting one metaphor and foregoing the other, and that mixed metaphors – the use of seemingly incompatible sources and/or targets within and between turns – are to be expected in such face-to-face talk despite the analytic inconvenience they seem to bring (Kimmel, 2010). They are also likely to conclude that metaphors play a meaningful role here because of how the dyad appears to be 'negotiating' their meanings in a natural and constructive way (Cameron & Maslen, 2010; Tay, 2016b, Tay 2017d). However, many practitioners would not consider this as convincing evidence that metaphors 'work' precisely because this negotiation cannot be reduced to clearly identifiable formal intervention(s) and measurable outcome(s), and therefore no causal mechanisms between the two can be demonstrated. McMullen (1996) describes the conflict between spontaneity and control most succinctly by noting that any attempt to dictate spontaneous talk by compelling people to (not) use metaphors "will not produce results of much value" (p. 250). This is not only because doing so is contradictory, but a controlled comparison of isolated metaphorical versus nonmetaphorical forms/structures fails to account for a large number of potential covariates that accompany the very act of metaphor use: therapist/client engagement, interest levels, and so on. On the other hand, however, the importance of imposing a reasonable level of control to ensure systematic and meaningful evaluations of metaphor-based therapy strategies remains key to evidence-based practice.

This section discusses some 'middle-path' approaches in research design and data analysis that aim at a reasonable balance between spontaneity and control, such that the findings could be meaningfully interpreted from both ends of the spectrum described here. The two approaches adopted in recent studies mentioned in the previous section (Tay, 2020a; Tay et al., 2019) can be seen as exemplifying two general research strategies in this context. The first strategy is to develop theoretically plausible 'middle-level' constructs that aim to accommodate the ideals and assumptions of both of the aforementioned research foci. The second strategy is to conduct research in psychotherapy contexts that have similar objectives but are different in nature than the prototypical therapist–client interactional setting. The present examples will show that many of these are inherently more suited to controlled experimentation without sacrificing spontaneity.

4.1 Communication Styles as a Middle-Level Construct

A middle-level construct is that which underpins experimentally feasible conditions of metaphor versus nonmetaphor use that are neither confined to delimited metaphorical forms/structures nor overly unconstrained in ways that prevent systematic comparison. One example is the notion of a 'metaphorical communication style,' defined as "the counselor introducing an overarching metaphor and probing its inferences for the target topic with the client in a spontaneous manner" (Tay, 2020a, p. 362). This idea of examining metaphor use as a (collaborative) response to an initial metaphorical conceptualization is theoretically consistent with many applications in the psychotherapy literature. For example, it dovetails with protocols where therapists are advised to notice client metaphors and guide them to develop their inferential potential step by step (Kopp & Craw, 1998; Sims & Whynot, 1997; Tay, 2012), and conceivably leads to productive 'metaphoric dances' (Mathieson et al., 2015a) wherein metaphors become part of a shared language between therapists and clients. It also redirects analytic attention away from specific source-target pairings often seen in the literature (e.g., difficulties as burdens, recovery as a journey) (Levitt et al., 2000; Sarpavaara & Koski-Jännes, 2013) and toward a more organic conception of metaphor use as a general communication strategy. Its counterpart can be described as a literal communication style. Under such a style, the same target topic is discussed without explicit appeal to an overarching metaphor, notwithstanding occasional metaphors for other topics that may arise. Any outcome measure(s) of interest could then be monitored across the duration of the target topic discussion, and used to compare the two styles afterwards.

The formal distinction between the two styles which defines them as comparable experimental conditions is thus the use of an initial metaphorical versus literal stimulus, or prompt, that is designed for the conversation to transit into spontaneous discussion of the target topic. The two prompts should ideally be checked for their equivalence in important aspects other than metaphoricity, such as understandability, naturalness, and familiarity (Cardillo et al., 2010), through an initial stimulus-matching and rating procedure. Participants would then be randomly assigned to either condition, ideally under the same therapist in both, and exposed to the stimulus after an opening period of interaction largely similar in both conditions. This reflects the classical experimental ideals of control and randomization. However, the spontaneous discussion that occurs after the prompt reflects the relatively unconstrained aspect of such a study design. There should be no attempt to control the metaphorical mappings and inferences, or how much of the discussion should comprise metaphorical language. The likely outcome might be discursively described as clusters of metaphorical language and other discourse markers such as signals and hedges that are known to co-occur with metaphors in conversation (Cameron & Deignan, 2003; Goatly, 1997; Tay, 2014). Likewise, there should be no deliberate attempt to avoid metaphors altogether in the literal style just because they are not focused on.

To illustrate the application of this middle-level construct, Tay (2020a) investigated the relative effects of a metaphorical versus literal communication style on the client's affective engagement levels. This was measured by their averaged skin conductance levels before and after the stimulus prompt, as briefly mentioned in the previous section. Figure 6 depicts the experimental trial process for each subject.

In this study, a trial begins with a five-minute habituation period, wherein clients are asked to relax and clear their minds. Their skin conductance levels are measured during this time but not subsequently analyzed. This practice is recommended for attaining baseline levels, detecting potential hyper- or hypo-responders, and to help clients get used to the environment (Braithwaite et al., 2015). The trial then formally begins with a five-minute pre-stimulus back-ground chat on the target topic of 'academic difficulties' (学习困难). This is labeled Period 1. After five minutes, the therapist transited into either the metaphorical stimulus *can you fully eat through the class* or the literal stimulus *can you fully understand the class*. Forty other constructed stimulus pairs were previously rated by another group of participants on key variables like how understandable, natural, familiar, similar in meaning, and metaphorical they were. A stimulus pair could only be used in the experiment if the metaphorical and literal stimulus differed significantly only in terms of metaphoricity. The time from stimulus presentation to the client's verbal response is labeled Period 2. After that, the therapist proceeded to guide the client through spontaneous interaction for another five minutes. This is Period 3, an extended response to

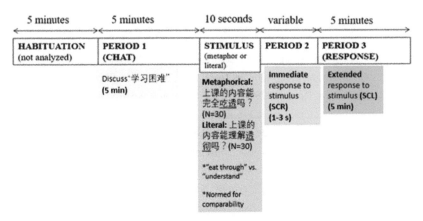

Figure 6 Experimental trial to compare communication styles

either the metaphorical or literal stimulus. Clients' skin conductance levels and verbal interaction with the therapist were monitored throughout, from Period 1 (prestimulus) to 3 (poststimulus).

As the previous section showed, clients generally displayed a higher increase in skin conductance from Period 1 to Period 3 under the metaphorical communication style. The immediate poststimulus response levels (Period 2) between styles were also compared, but will not be discussed here. The more pertinent point is that the design allows for further comparison of the linguistic and discursive features that spontaneously unfold across both styles – as a type of outcome in itself, and/or as potential correlates of skin conductance change. For example, the present study found that (i) the metaphorical condition generated more words related to the target topic, (ii) the metaphorical condition had a higher number of conversational turns, and (iii) clients in the metaphorical condition spoke more words than those in the literal condition. Additionally, changes in skin conductance levels were positively correlated with the use of source domain words, metaphor signals, and markers of uncertainty. All these results collectively point toward the potential of the overarching metaphor to facilitate greater client output and dialogic interaction, and the possibility that engaging with the metaphor (via source domain terms and metaphor signals) drives affective engagement. These analyses are made possible by the nature of the study design, which can be replicated with appropriate modifications to other similar contexts.

4.2 Beyond the Prototypical Therapist–Client Talk

An important reason why linguists develop an interest in psychotherapy is its popular conception as a mental healthcare activity constituted by linguistic interaction (Ferrara, 1991, 1994; Peräkylä et al., 2011). This makes it easier, for pragmatic purposes, to demonstrate the potential value of linguistic analysis. Psychotherapy, however, is far from an exclusively verbal activity. We may, for instance, wish to consider related settings, such as therapist supervision and training workshops, as potential sites for metaphor research (Aronov & Brodsky, 2009; Rosenbaum & Ronen, 1998; Tay, 2011). Even if we limit ourselves to forms of therapist–client interaction, there are many therapeutic innovations and practices that complement, co-occur with, or even replace the prototypical verbal mode. Much has been written about how expressive modalities such as music, art, and dance (Bruscia, 1998; Wittig & Davis, 2012) could be especially beneficial for particular therapist and client groups. Such forms of creative expression and interpretation may help reduce distressing psychological symptoms, give clients an alternative to conventional norms and expectations of verbal interaction, and be more relevant for clients with body-related psychopathology (Röhricht, 2009). More important for the present purpose, metaphors naturally occur in many of these settings and could afford overlooked opportunities for more controlled research designs that do not come at the price of spontaneity.

An example of a creative therapeutic approach is to use visual images as a tool to help therapists and clients gain insight into the situation at hand. The images may range from photographs of actual people and objects to abstract illustrations that do not have any obvious meaning at first glance. This approach has been referred to as 'phototherapy' or picture-based counseling (Ginicola et al., 2012; Stevens & Spears, 2009). Either the therapist or the client may choose the images (Star & Cox, 2008), and there is no prescribed method or technique for how best to use them. Images may, for example, be used to build rapport, identify symptoms, present problems, explore thoughts and emotions, or even as spiritual/religious symbols to inspire clients. A crucial common point among these applications, however, is that the image and the associated activity is often strategically introduced at some point within a session as a break or 'relief' that is nevertheless still relevant to the objectives of the surrounding talk. Consider the following two authentic examples which show how the therapist introduces an image in the midst of their spontaneous interaction.

> 来，我们现在先不说这个。我给你看这张图，你生活中有没有这样类似的一些经历？见过的或者是发生在你身上的？ Come, let us not talk about this for now. I'll show you a picture. Do you have life experiences similar to what you see in this picture? What you've witnessed or experienced?
> 我们现在暂停一下，来个小活动。我这里有一张图片，你看了这张图片之后，你自己想个小故事，随意，你自己发挥想 象力 Let's pause for a while and have a small activity. Here is a picture, look at it and think of a small story. Do as you like, use your imagination.

In both cases, the therapist and client had been discussing difficulties with adjusting to life in university. The therapist then explicitly suspends the topic by asking the client to "not talk about this for now" and "pause for a while and have a small activity." He proceeds to introduce the picture and invite the client to relate it to "similar life experiences" or "imagine a small story." The picture shows a frustrated man next to his broken-down car beside a long road, which has no inherent 'literal' link with the previous topic of university life. From the therapist's perspective, this can provide relief by shifting attention away from the client and onto some external object (Ginicola et al., 2012). Returning to the researcher's dilemma between spontaneity and control, the strategic in-session use of images could also be seen as initiating a more controlled activity that temporarily suspends, but does not contradict, the purpose of the broader spontaneous interaction.

It would therefore be possible to devise naturalistic conditions for comparing the processes and outcomes of metaphorical versus other modes of picture interpretation. The two spontaneous examples given here somewhat reflect this possibility. In the first case, the therapist alludes to the target topic of "similar life experiences," which might prompt clients to use the picture as a metaphorical source domain, mapping themselves to the man, their situation to the car, and so on. This contrasts with the second case, wherein the client is simply asked to "do as you like." In another previous study on affective engagement (Tay et al., 2019), a third 'literal condition' was added wherein participants were prompted to simply describe a picture in literal terms. The results of that study suggested that a metaphorical mode of elaboration was indeed more affectively engaging. Different ways of inviting clients to interpret the picture therefore comprised the controlled independent variable, but they were free to do so in whatever way and for however long they wanted afterward. The study leaned more toward control than spontaneity by using a within-subjects design outside of an actual counseling context, wherein all participants interpreted the picture under all three conditions in counterbalanced sequence. However, it would also be plausible to conduct similar studies in actual sessions using a between-subjects design without compromising spontaneity. This is precisely because the therapist can select an appropriate moment to introduce the activity using the topic-suspending prompts as illustrated earlier. Increased awareness of such strategic but lesser-known interventions that are at the same time conducive for systematic research would offer linguists considerably more opportunities to study the holistic nature and effectiveness of metaphors in psychotherapy.

5 Summary

This work offered a reflection on lessons learned from long-term collaboration between a linguistics-trained metaphor researcher and psychotherapists interested in metaphor. Collaborative work between academics and industry partners is becoming an increasingly important indicator of research impact in the humanities and social sciences. While researcher–practitioner collaboration can take on many different forms, as highlighted in the Introduction, this work aimed to provide focused advice for beginning researchers who are looking to navigate the realities of collaborative research in psychotherapy. Specific attention was paid to each of the three foundational components of psychotherapy: the therapist, the client, and the interactional setting. We first considered how linguists could build common ground and maximize their collaboration with therapists by engaging them in more meaningful ways along the typical research trajectory. This includes working together on mater-ials and stimulus design, inviting therapists as experimental confederates, and involving them in the data analysis process through a systematic procedure I have elsewhere called 'correspondent analysis.' We then confronted questions about client variability in use, understanding, and, perhaps most importantly, appreciation of metaphor. These are critical yet overlooked questions because of the tension between accounts that paint an ideal picture of metaphor effective-ness with limited empirical evidence, and the ideals of 'patient-centeredness' that ostensibly see things through the patient's eye. We discussed how variabil-ity in client responses to metaphor manifests in self-apparent as well as latent ways across different psychotherapy contexts. The key point is to model such variability as explicitly as possible, instead of controlling or relegating it to the realm of research limitations, as is often done. Lastly, we reflected on the conflict between spontaneity and control that lies at the heart of empirical research on psychotherapy talk, and how it affects the case of metaphor. Research foci at both ends of the spectrum, exemplified respectively by dis-course analysis and randomized controlled trials, could be brought closer by developing middle-level constructs that address the interests and accommodate the weaknesses of either. Linguists can also discover more research opportun-ities by recognizing possibilities beyond the prototypical scenario of therapist–client interaction. A case in point is the practice of picture-based counseling, the very nature of which allows relatively controlled investigation embedded within a spontaneous context.

5.1 The Therapist, the Client, and the Setting in Interaction

The three components were discussed one at a time from Sections 2 to 4, but in reality it is unlikely that linguists would be dealing with any of them in isolation. An important question in its own right that is beyond the scope of the present work is how these components might interact in specific ways to influence our methodological and analytical decisions. Some of these are due to inherent confounds beyond easy reach of researchers and therapists alike, such as how therapists and clients inevitably and constantly shape each other's attitudes and perspectives. However, others can be regarded as possibilities or opportunities to be anticipated at the initial stages of conceptualizing a collaborative project. We will briefly discuss some examples here. Firstly, the modeling of client variability in metaphor-related responses (Section 3) could itself be a subject of collaborative correspondent analysis with therapists (Section 2). These aspects were independently treated in the present work: the former by using qualitative and quantitative models from the researcher's perspective alone; the latter in a more general sense without necessarily involving client response data. Recall that correspondent analysis as defined in Section 2 involves (i) the therapist identifying and annotating transcript portions that reflect important therapeutic processes, (ii) the linguist doing the same for phenomena of interest, such as metaphors in this case, and (iii) intersecting the two to identify overlaps and/or juxtapositions that could lead to further insight. Applying this in the context of client response data – for example, the idiosyncratic patterns of affective engagement with metaphor discussed in Section 3 – therapists' 'annotation' of the statistical variability between subjects (Figure 4) might take the form of potential explanations, derived from theory and experience, for specific change patterns from Phase 1 to Phase 3. These include differences between sharp and gentle rises/falls, as well as cases where affective levels remain constant throughout. Such an approach also highlights the importance of harnessing 'substantive expertise' or domain knowledge (Conway, 2010) in data analysis in applied contexts.

The second example is to engage therapists in the design of so-called middle-level constructs (Section 4), even though the latter might appear to be a research technicality. Our example of metaphorical versus literal 'communication styles' is a case in point. We defined a metaphorical communication style as the therapist "introducing an overarching metaphor and probing its inferences for the target topic with the client in a spontaneous manner," and the corresponding literal communication style as equivalent except for the absence of an overarching metaphor. Although these styles were deemed to be consistent with many applications in the literature, it is important to acknowledge that their formulation is mainly motivated by the requirements of basic research design, such as having two (or more) conditions that are defined by specific formal stimuli and that only differ along the specified independent variable. The standard research practice of checking these conditions using ratings from subjects could be significantly enriched by involving therapists in the process. Issues such as whether the styles are realistic or authentic from a practical rather than research point of view still need to be considered with reference to therapists' input. It is easy to overlook this point because the very notion of middle-level constructs was supposed to address the inherent conflict between research and practice, but how this conflict itself is understood by therapists should not be neglected.

Lastly, interactions between the components can also be conceptualized in terms of how issues relating to therapists and clients mutually apply. Two possibilities were briefly considered in Sections 3 and 4. The first is the idea of extending therapist–researcher collaboration to client–researcher collaboration, one example being the notion of 'correspondent analysis' with client-driven analytical perspectives. The second possibility is to extend the focus on client variability to therapist variability in metaphor responses. As explained, these extensions are relatively less exigent in the current research landscape, but are promising ideas for future work.

5.2 Navigating Other Contexts of Collaborative Metaphor Research

To conclude, some thoughts will be offered on how the present reflective approach might also be useful in other contexts of collaborative applied metaphor research. Two prominent examples where metaphor research has a salient applied dimension, and researchers are increasingly engaging professionals in their work, are the fields of education and advertising. Table 5 is a summary depiction of psychotherapy, education, and advertising along the parameters that define the present reflective approach: the professionals; the targets of their products and services; and the nature, media, and processes that characterize each context.

This work presented the case of psychotherapy and called for deeper engagement with therapists, keener awareness of varied client responses to metaphor, and a more flexible mindset in dealing with the inherent conditions of therapy. A broadly similar approach could be taken when reflecting on metaphor research in educational settings, which has been prominent across various subject areas and continues to move in promising new directions (Ahlgren et al., 2021). The parallels between psychotherapy and teaching, and the idea of therapy as education, have long been noted (Tharp, 1999). Teachers impart knowledge and develop their students in somewhat similar ways as therapists for clients, and thus presently discussed notions like collaborative stimulus design, experimentation, data analysis, and client variability each has noteworthy analogues in the education context. Just like therapists, teachers may be consulted for designing instruments and interventions, can serve as confederate experimenters in the classroom[, and participate in correspondent analysis of data. Relevant data in educational settings is also likely to be more diverse in form and function than psychotherapy, ranging from classroom discourse to teaching materials and student assessments. Just like psychotherapy, however, research has tended to proceed under the optimistic assumption that metaphors 'work,' and student variability in attitudes and responses to metaphors is still overlooked. It is more common for researchers to use metaphor as a tool to explore students' attitudes and beliefs about the subject matter instead (Güner, 2012; Wan, 2014). The one-to-many setting of the typical classroom, compared to one-to-one therapy settings, should provide further room for researchers to critically reflect on how to model such variability. Inherent conditions of the classroom and therapy room also differ in some respect. The rich tradition of (quasi)-experimental education research (Gopalan et al., 2020) might imply that researchers interested in testing the effectiveness of metaphor would face less of a dilemma between spontaneity and control but, just like psychotherapy, many opportunities for researching metaphor are available outside the prototypical classroom context. Professional development workshops are a good example where metaphor-related interventions, techniques, etc., can be tested in systematic and creative ways (Loads, 2010).

Another prime example of collaborative applied metaphor research is in the domain of advertising (Pérez Sobrino et al., 2021). It is encouraging to see increasing mainstream recognition of joint projects between advertising agencies and metaphor researchers. The collaboration between researchers at the University of Birmingham and marketing communications agency Big Cat, for instance, bagged the 'Partnership of the Year' award at the Birmingham Post's Business Awards 2018. It nevertheless seems that many metaphor-related studies that analyze and/or deploy advertisements as stimuli still tend to either use existing ones, or to construct them according to the requirements of the study design (Forceville, 1996; Landau et al., 2015; Littlemore et al., 2018). Although there might be good practical reasons for doing so, it would be worth reflecting on the extent to which direct professional input in the development of study designs, stimuli, and other materials is beneficial. Unlike psychotherapy, consumer feedback (on metaphor) and its variability across demographics is already a well-established line of empirical research (Jeong, 2008; Landau et al., 2015). Recent studies have also critically reflected upon how the unique nature, media, and processes of advertising compel new ways of thinking about metaphor research and application. For example, the relatively short time span of advertisements and the lack of immediate recipient feedback implies that metaphors should be neither too simplistic nor too complex (Burgers et al., 2015). The necessity of considering how metaphors in advertisements interact with other tropes like metonymy, irony, and hyperbole (Burgers et al., 2015; Pérez Sobrino et al., 2019) has also been highlighted. Since many metaphors tend to be ephemeral in advertisements that are themselves short, more critical questions, such as whether consumers are even likely to notice them, have also been asked (Pan & Tay, 2022). Furthermore, the field of advertising introduces the nuance that product makers and service providers may be regarded as both 'professionals' and 'targets' according to Table 5. On the one hand, they are ultimately responsible for the message to be communicated to consumers, but on the other hand, they are also clients receiving input about their message from advertising agencies.

Table 5 Summary depiction of collaborative applied metaphor research contexts

Context	Professionals	Targets	Nature, media, and processes
Psychotherapy	Therapists	Clients	Spontaneous verbal interaction in a mostly face-to-face and one-to-one setting
Education	Teachers	Students	Spontaneous and planned multimodal interaction both virtually and face-to-face, in a mostly one-to-many setting
Advertising	Advertisers Product makers and service providers	Consumers	Mostly planned multimodal one-way, one-to-many communication in virtual settings

While it is not difficult to outline these broad conceptual similarities between different domains and offer some general pointers, successful navigation still requires actual exposure to and experience in a specific domain. The opportunities and potential pitfalls highlighted for the case of psychotherapy in the present work may therefore not fully apply elsewhere, and it would be up to other researchers with relevant experience to offer a similar reflection. In conclusion, metaphor researchers working in virtually any context of collaborative research should aspire to show the benefits of their research for the corresponding social activities. It is hoped that this work can support the aspirations of researchers interested in the psychotherapy context, through systematic reflection on how on-the-ground realities should be allowed to shape research. Only then can applied metaphor research be truly considered collaborative, and useful for researchers and practitioners alike.

References

Ahlgren, K., Golden, A., & Magnusson, U. (2021). Metaphor in Education. A Multilingual Perspective [Special Issue]. *Metaphor and the Social World*, 11(2).

Anderson, H., & Goolishian, H. (1988). Human systems as linguistic systems: Preliminary and evolving ideas about the implications for clinical theory. *Family Process*, 27(4), 371–393.

Anderson, M. (2003). Embodied cognition: A field guide. *Artificial Intelligence*, *149*, 91–130.

Angus, L. E., & Korman, Y. (2002). A metaphor theme analysis: Conflicts, coherence and change in brief psychotherapy. In S. R. Fussell, ed., *The Verbal Communication of Emotions: Interdisciplinary Perspectives*. Mahwah, NJ: Lawrence Erlbaum, pp. 151–165.

Antaki, C., Barnes, R., & Leudar, I. (2005). Diagnostic formulations in psychotherapy. *Discourse Studies*, 7(6), 627–647.

Aronov, N. E., & Brodsky, S. L. (2009). The river model: A metaphor and tool for training new psychotherapists. *Journal of Contemporary Psychotherapy*, 39, 187–195.

Association for Psychological Science. (2009). Where's the science? The sorry state of psychotherapy. *ScienceDaily*, October 3rd. www.sciencedaily.com/releases/2009/10/091002182633.htm.

Attkisson, C. C., & Zwick, R. (1982). The client satisfaction questionnaire. *Evaluation and Program Planning*, 5(3), 233–237.

Barlow, M., & Kemmer, S. (2002). *Usage Based Models of Language*. Stanford, CA: CSLI Publications.

Beck, A. T. (1976). *Cognitive Therapy and the Emotional Disorders*. New York: International Universities Press.

Blenkiron, P. (2010). *Stories and Analogies in Cognitive Behaviour Therapy*. Chichester: John Wiley & Sons.

Boeynaems, A., Burgers, C., Konijn, E. A., & Steen, G. J. (2017). The effects of metaphorical framing on political persuasion: A systematic literature review. *Metaphor and Symbol*, 32(2), 118–134.

Boles, L. (1998). Conversational discourse analysis as a method for evaluating progress in aphasia: A case report. *Journal of Communication Disorders*, 31 (3), 261–273.

Bos, J. (2020). *Research Ethics for Students in the Social Sciences*. Cham: Springer.

Braithwaite, J., Watson, D., Jones, R., & Rowe, M. (2015). *A Guide for Analysing Electrodermal Activity (EDA) & Skin Conductance Responses (SCRs) for Psychological Experiments*. Birmingham: SAAL.

Bruscia, K. E. (1998). *Defining Music Therapy*, 2nd ed. Gilsum, NH: Barcelona Publishers.

Bucholtz, M. (2021). Community-centered collaboration in applied linguistics. *Applied Linguistics*, 42(6), 1153–1161.

Burgers, C., Konijn, E. A., Steen, G. J., & Iepsma, M. A. R. (2015). Making ads less complex, yet more creative and persuasive: The effects of conventional metaphors and irony in print advertising. *International Journal of Advertising*, 34(3), 515–532.

Cameron, L., & Deignan, A. (2003). Combining large and small corpora to investigate tuning devices around metaphor in spoken discourse. *Metaphor and Symbol*, 18(3), 149–160.

Cameron, L., & Maslen, R. (2010). *Metaphor Analysis*. London: Equinox.

Cardillo, E. R., Schmidt, G. L., Kranjec, A., & Chatterjee, A. (2010). Stimulus design is an obstacle course: 560 matched literal and metaphorical sentences for testing neural hypotheses about metaphor. *Behavior Research Methods*, 42(3), 651–664.

Carlsen, M. B. (1996). Metaphor, meaning-making, and metamorphosis. In K. T. Kuehlwei, ed., *Constructing Realities: Meaning-Making Perspectives for Psychotherapists*. San Francisco, CA: Jossey-Bass, pp. 337–367.

Caruth, E., & Ekstein, R. (1966). Interpretation within the metaphor: Further considerations. *Journal of the American Academy of Child Psychiatry*, 5(1), 35–45.

Cirillo, L., & Crider, C. (1995). Distinctive therapeutic uses of metaphor. *Psychotherapy*, 32, 511–519.

Citron, F., & Goldberg, A. (2014). Metaphorical sentences are more emotionally engaging than their literal counterparts. *Journal of Cognitive Neuroscience*, 26(11), 2585–2595.

Conway, D. (2010). *The Data Science Venn Diagram*. blog.revolutionanalytics.com.

Coulthard, M. (2010). Forensic linguistics: The application of language description in legal contexts. *Langage et Societe*, 132(2), 15–33.

Coupé, C. (2018). Modeling linguistic variables with regression models: Addressing non-Gaussian distributions, non-independent observations, and non-linear predictors with random effects and generalized additive models for location, scale, and shape. *Frontiers in Psychology*, 9(Apr.), 1–21.

Craske, M. G., Niles, A. N., Burklund, L. J. et al. (2014). Randomized controlled trial of cognitive behavioral therapy and acceptance and commitment therapy for social phobia: Outcomes and moderators. *Journal of Consulting and Clinical Psychology*, 82(6), 1034–1048.

Currier, J. M., Holland, J. M., & Neimeyer, R. A. (2006). Sense making, grief and the experience of violent loss: Toward a mediational model. *Death Studies*, 30, 403–428.

Dawson, M. E., Schell, A. M., & Filion, D. L. (2007). The electrodermal system. In J. Cacioppo, L. Tassinary, & G. Berntson, eds., *Handbook of Psychophysiology*, 3rd edn. New York: Cambridge University Press, pp. 159–181.

Demjén, Z., & Semino, E. (2020). Communicating nuanced results in language consultancy: The case of cancer and the violence metaphor. In L. Mullany, ed., *Professional Communication*. Cham: Palgrave Macmillan, pp. 191–210.

Dwairy, M. (1999). Toward psycho-cultural approach in Middle Eastern societies. *Clinical Psychology Review*, 19(8), 909–915.

Dwairy, M. (2009). Culture analysis and metaphor psychotherapy with Arab-Muslim clients. *Journal of Clinical Psychology*, 65(2), 199–209.

Dyer, C., & Joseph, S. (2006). What is an RCT? *Counselling & Psychotherapy Research*, 6(4), 264–265.

Edelson, J. T. (1983). Freud's use of metaphor. *The Psychoanalytic Study of the Child*, 38(1), 17–59.

Evans, V., & Green, M. (2006). *Cognitive Linguistics: An Introduction*. Edinburgh: Edinburgh University Press.

Ferrara, K. W. (1991). Accommodation in therapy. In H. Giles, J. Coupland, & N. Coupland, eds., *Contexts of Accommodation*. Cambridge: Cambridge University Press, pp. 187–222.

Ferrara, K. W. (1994). *Therapeutic Ways with Words*. Oxford Studies in Sociolinguistics. New York: Oxford University Press.

Finger, S. C., Elliott, J. E., & Remer, R. (1993). Simulation as a tool in family therapy research. *Journal of Family Therapy*, 15(4), 365–379.

Forceville, C. (1996). *Pictorial Metaphor in Advertising*. London: Routledge.

Forceville, C., & Urios-Aparisi, E. (2009). *Multimodal Metaphor*. Berlin: Mouton de Gruyter.

Foulks, E., Persons, J., & Merkel, R. (1986). The effect of patients' beliefs about their illnesses on compliance in psychotherapy. *American Journal of Psychiatry*, 143(3), 340–344.

Frank, R. M. (2008). Introduction: Sociocultural situatedness. In R. M. Frank, R. Dirven, T. Ziemke, & E. Bernárdez, eds., *Body, Language and Mind. Volume 2: Sociocultural Situatedness*. Berlin: Mouton de Gruyter, pp. 1–18.

Fuoli, M., & Hart, C. (2018). Trust-building strategies in corporate discourse: An experimental study. *Discourse and Society*, 29(5), 514–552.

Furbee, N. L., & Stanley, L. A. (2002). A collaborative model for preparing indigenous curators of a heritage language. *International Journal of the Sociology of Language*, 2002(154), 113–128.

Geeraerts, D., Kristiansen, G., & Peirsman, Y. (2010). *Advances in Cognitive Sociolinguistics*. Berlin:Mouton de Gruyter.

Gelo, O. C. G., & Mergenthaler, E. (2012). Unconventional metaphors and emotional-cognitive regulation in a metacognitive interpersonal therapy. *Psychotherapy Research*, 22(2), 159–175.

Gerber, S., & Gurland, G. (1989). Applied pragmatics in the assessment of aphasia. *Seminars in Speech and Language*, 10(4), 263–281.

Gibbs, R. W. (1996). Why many concepts are metaphorical. *Cognition*, 61(3), 309–319.

Gibbs, R. W. (2010). The wonderful, chaotic, creative, heroic, challenging world of researching and applying metaphor: A celebration of the past and some peeks into the future. In G. Low, Z. Todd, A. Deignan, & L. Cameron, eds., *Researching and Applying Metaphor in the Real World*. Amsterdam: John Benjamins, pp. 1–18.

Gibbs, R. W., & Siman, J. (2021). How we resist metaphors. *Language and Cognition*, 13(4), 670–692.

Ginicola, M. M., Smith, C., & Trzaska, J. (2012). Counseling through images: Using photography to guide the counseling process and achieve treatment goals. *Journal of Creativity in Mental Health*, 7(4), 310–329.

Gino, F., Ayal, S., & Ariely, D. (2009). Contagion and differentiation in unethical behavior: The effect of one bad apple on the barrel. *Psychological Science*, 20 (3), 393–398.

Glucksberg, S. (2003). The psycholinguistics of metaphor. *Trends in Cognitive Sciences*, 7(2), 92–96.

Glucksberg, S., & McGlone, M. S. (1999). When love is not a journey: What metaphors mean. *Journal of Pragmatics*, 31(12), 1541–1558.

Glucksman, M., Quinlan, D., & Leigh, H. (1985). Skin conductance changes and psychotherapeutic content in the treatment of a phobic patient. *British Journal of Medical Psychology*, 58, 155–163.

Goatly, A. (1997). *The Language of Metaphors*. London: Routledge.

Goldberg, R. M., & Stephenson, J. B. (2016). Staying with the metaphor: Applying reality therapy's use of metaphors to grief counseling. *Journal of Creativity in Mental Health*, 11(1), 105–117.

Gopalan, M., Rosinger, K., & Ahn, J. B. (2020). Use of quasi-experimental research designs in education research: Growth, promise, and challenges. *Review of Research in Education*, 44(1), 218–243.

Grady, J. (1997). *Foundations of Meaning: Primary Metaphors and Primary Scenes*. Berkerley: University of California.

Grant, J., & Crawley, J. (2002). *Transference and Projection*. Buckingham: Open University Press.

Greenberg, R. P., Constantino, M. J., & Bruce, N. (2006). Are patient expectations still relevant for psychotherapy process and outcome? *Clinical Psychology Review*, 26(6), 657–678.

Grice, H. P. (1975). Logic and conversation. In P. Cole & J. L. Morgan, eds., *Syntax and Semantics Vol 3*. New York: Academic Press, pp. 41–58.

Güner, N. (2012). Using metaphor analysis to explore high school students' attitudes towards learning mathematics. *Education*, 1, 39–48.

Hamakawa, N., Kogetsu, A., Isono, M. et al. (2021). The practice of active patient involvement in rare disease research using ICT: Experiences and lessons from the RUDY JAPAN project. *Research Involvement and Engagement*, 7(1), 9.

Harrison, X. A., Donaldson, L., Correa-Cano, M. E. et al. (2018). A brief introduction to mixed effects modelling and multi-model inference in ecology. *PeerJ*, 6(e4794).

Heck, R., & Thomas, S. (2015). *An Introduction to Multilevel Modeling Techniques*. New York: Routledge.

Heritage, J. (1984). *Garfinkel and Ethnomethodology*. Cambridge: Polity Press.

Hodgson, J. L., Lamson, A. L., & Feldhousen, E. B. (2007). Use of simulated clients in marriage and family therapy education. *Journal of Marital and Family Therapy*, 33(1), 35–50.

Holdsworth, E., Bowen, E., Brown, S., & Howat, D. (2014). Client engagement in psychotherapeutic treatment and associations with client characteristics, therapist characteristics, and treatment factors. *Clinical Psychology Review*, 34(5), 428–450.

Hooghe, A., Neimeyer, R. A., & Rober, P. (2012). "Cycling around an emotional core of sadness": Emotion regulation in a couple after the loss of a child. *Qualitative Health Research*, 22(9), 1220–1231.

Horvath, A., & Greenberg, L. (1994). *The Working Alliance: Theory, Research and Practice*. New York: John Wiley & Sons.

Israel, M. (2015). *Research Ethics and Integrity for Social Scientists*, 2nd ed., Thousand Oaks,CA: Sage.

Javaid, M. K., Forestier-Zhang, L., Watts, L. et al. (2016). The RUDY study platform: A novel approach to patient driven research in rare musculoskeletal diseases. *Orphanet Journal of Rare Diseases*, 11(1), 150.

Jeong, S. (2008). Visual metaphor in advertising: Is the persuasive effect attributable to visual argumentation or metaphorical rhetoric? *Journal of Marketing Communications*, 14(1), 59–73.

Johnson, M. (1987). *The Body in the Mind: The Bodily Basis of Meaning, Imagination and Reason.* Chicago: University of Chicago Press.

Kaplonyi, J., Bowles, K.-A., Nestel, D. et al. (2017). Understanding the impact of simulated patients on health care learners' communication skills: A systematic review. *Medical Education*, 51(12), 1209–1219.

Kimmel, M. (2010). Why we mix metaphors (and mix them well): Discourse coherence, conceptual metaphor, and beyond. *Journal of Pragmatics*, 42(1), 97–115.

Kimmel, M. (2012). Optimizing the analysis of metaphor in discourse: How to make the most of qualitative software and find a good research design. *Review of Cognitive Linguistics*, 10(1), 1–48.

Kopp, R. R., & Craw, M. J. (1998). Metaphoric language, metaphoric cognition, and cognitive therapy. *Psychotherapy*, 35(3), 306–311.

Kövecses, Z. (2005). *Metaphor in Culture: Universality and Variation.* Cambridge: Cambridge University Press.

Kövecses, Z. (2020). *Extended Conceptual Metaphor Theory.* Cambirdge: Cambridge University Press.

Kuhlen, A. K., & Brennan, S. E. (2013). Language in dialogue: When confederates might be hazardous to your data. *Psychonomic Bulletin and Review*, 20 (1), 54–72.

Labov, W. (1984). Field methods of the project on linguistic change and variation. In J. Baugh & J. Sherzer, eds., *Language in Use: Readings in sociolinguistics*. Englewood: Prentice-Hall, pp. 28–53.

Laine, C., & Davidoff, F. (1996). Patient-centered medicine. A professional evolution. *JAMA*, 275(2), 152–156.

Lakoff, G. (1993). The contemporary theory of metaphor. In A. Ortony, ed., *Metaphor and Thought*, 2nd ed. Cambridge: Cambridge University Press, pp. 202–251.

Lakoff, G., & Johnson, M. (1980). *Metaphors We Live By.* Chicago: University of Chicago Press.

Lakoff, G., & Johnson, M. (1999). *Philosophy in the Flesh: The Embodied Mind and its Challenges to Western Thought.* New York: Basic Books.

Landau, M. J., Nelson, N. M., & Keefer, L. A. (2015). Divergent effects of metaphoric company logos: Do they convey what the company does or what I need? *Metaphor and Symbol*, 30(4), 314–338.

Lane, C., & Rollnick, S. (2007). The use of simulated patients and role-play in communication skills training: A review of the literature to August 2005. *Patient Education and Counseling*, 67(1), 13–20.

Lankton, S., & Lankton, C. H. (1983). *The Answer Within: A Clinical Framework of Ericksonian Hypnotherapy.* New York: Brunnel/Mazel.

Levin, F. M. (1980). Metaphor, affect, and arousal: How interpretations might work. *The Annual of Psychoanalysis*, 8, 231–245.

Levinson, S. C. (1983). *Pragmatics*. Cambridge: Cambridge University Press.

Levitt, H., Korman, Y., & Angus, L. (2000). A metaphor analysis in treatments of depression: Metaphor as a marker of change. *Counselling Psychology Quarterly*, 13(1), 23–35.

Littlemore, J., Sobrino, P. P., Houghton, D., Shi, J., & Winter, B. (2018). What makes a good metaphor? A cross-cultural study of computer-generated metaphor appreciation. *Metaphor and Symbol*, 33(2), 101–122.

Littlemore, J., & Turner, S. (2019). What can metaphor tell us about experiences of pregnancy loss and how are these experiences reflected in midwife practice? *Frontiers in Communication*, 4 (August), https://doi.org/10.3389/fcomm.2019.00042.

Loads, D. (2010). "I'm a dancer" and "I've got a saucepan stuck on my head": Metaphor in helping lecturers to develop being-for-uncertainty. *Teaching in Higher Education*, 15(4), 409–421.

Long, M. (1983). Native speaker/non-native speaker conversation and the negotiation of comprehensible input. *Applied Linguistics*, 4(2), 126–141.

Low, G., Todd, Z., Deignan, A., & Cameron, L. (2010). *Researching and Applying Metaphor in the Real World*. Amsterdam: John Benjamins.

Lyddon, W. J., Clay, A. L., & Sparks, C. L. (2001). Metaphor and change in counselling. *Journal of Counseling & Development*, 79(3), 269–274.

Marci, C. D., Ham, J., Moran, E., & Orr, S. P. (2007). Physiologic correlates of perceived therapist empathy and social-emotional process during psychotherapy. *The Journal of Nervous and Mental Disease*, 195(2), 103–111.

Marks, S., Mathie, E., Smiddy, J., Jones, J., & da Silva-Gane, M. (2018). Reflections and experiences of a co-researcher involved in a renal research study. *Research Involvement and Engagement*, 4, 36–46.

Martin, S. (2010). Co-production of social research: Strategies for engaged scholarship. *Public Money & Management*, 30(4), 211–218.

Mathieson, F., Jordan, J., Carter, J. D., & Stubbe, M. (2015a). The metaphoric dance: Co-construction of metaphor in cognitive behaviour therapy. *The Cognitive Behaviour Therapist*, 8, e24.

Mathieson, F., Jordan, J., Carter, J., & Stubbe, M. (2015b). Nailing down metaphors in CBT: Definition, identification and frequency. *Behavioural and Cognitive Psychotherapy*, 44(2), 236–248.

Matthews, D., Lieven, E., & Tomasello, M. (2010). What's in a manner of speaking? Children's sensitivity to partner-specific referential precedents. *Developmental Psychology*, 46(4), 749–760.

Matthews, M., Gay, G., & Doherty, G. (2014). Taking part: Role-play in the design of therapeutic systems. *Proceedings of the SIGCHI Conference on Human Factors in Computing Systems*, 643–652.

McGlone, M. S. (2007). What is the explanatory value of a conceptual metaphor? *Language & Communication*, 27, 109–126.

McMullen, L. M. (1996). Studying the use of figurative language in psychotherapy: The search for researchable questions. *Metaphor and Symbolic Activity*, 11(4), 241–255.

McMullen, L. M. (2008). Putting it in context: Metaphor and psychotherapy. In R. W. Gibbs, ed., *The Cambridge Handbook of Metaphor and Thought*. Cambridge: Cambridge University Press, pp. 397–411.

McWhinney, I. R. (1993). Why we need a new clinical method. *Scandinavian Journal of Primary Health Care*, 11(1), 3–7.

Mead, N., & Bower, P. (2000). Patient-centredness: A conceptual framework and review of the empirical literature. *Social Science and Medicine*, 51(7), 1087–1110.

Mondada, L. (2010). Therapy interactions: Specific genre or "blown up" version of ordinary conversational practices? *Pragmatics*, 8(2), 155–165.

Moradveisi, L., Huibers, M., Renner, F., & Arntz, A. (2014). The influence of patients' preference/attitude towards psychotherapy and antidepressant medication on the treatment of major depressive disorder. *Journal of Behavior Therapy and Experimental Psychiatry*, 45(1), 170–177.

Morris, N. (2015). Providing ethical guidance for collaborative research in developing countries. *Research Ethics*, 11(4), 211–235.

Murphy, G. L. (1997). Reasons to doubt the present evidence for metaphoric representation. *Cognition*, 62(1), 99–108.

Murtaugh, P. A. (2007). Simplicity and complexity in ecological data analysis. *Ecology*, 88(1), 56–62.

Musolff, A. (2012). The study of metaphor as part of critical discourse analysis. *Critical Discourse Studies*, 9(3), 301–310.

Nadeau, J. W. (2006). Metaphorically speaking: The use of metaphors in grief therapy. *Illness Crisis and Loss*, 14(3), 201–221.

Nathan, P. E. (1996). Validated forms of psychotherapy may lead to better-validated psychotherapy. *Clinical Psychology: Science and Practice*, 3(3), 251–255.

Neimeyer, R. A., & Mahoney, M. J. (1995). *Constructivism in Psychotherapy*. Washington, DC: American Psychological Association.

Neimeyer, R. A., & Thompson, B. E. (2014). Meaning making and the art of grief therapy. In B. E. Thompson & R. A. Neimeyer, eds., *Grief and the*

Expressive Arts: Practices for Creating Meaning. New York: Routledge, pp. 3–13.

Nestel, D., & Tierney, T. (2007). Role-play for medical students learning about communication: Guidelines for maximising benefits. *BMC Medical Education*, 7(1), 3.

Norcross, J. C. (1990). An eclectic definition of psychotherapy. In J. K. Zeig & W. M. Munion, eds., *What is Psychotherapy? Contemporary Perspectives*. San Francisco: Jossey-Bass, pp. 218–220.

Nyström, M. E., Karltun, J., Keller, C., & Andersson Gäre, B. (2018). Collaborative and partnership research for improvement of health and social services: Researcher's experiences from 20 projects. *Health Research Policy and Systems*, 16(1), 46.

Pan, M. X., & Tay, D. (2022). Individual differences in identifying creative metaphors from video ads. *Metaphor and the Social World*, 13 (1). https://doi.org/10.1075/msw.20016.pan.

Peräkylä, A., Antaki, C., Vehviläinen, S., & Leudar, I. (2011). *Conversation Analysis and Psychotherapy*. Cambridge: Cambridge University Press.

Pérez Sobrino, P., Littlemore, J., & Ford, S. (2021). *Unpacking Creativity: The Power of Figurative Communication in Advertising*. Cambridge: Cambridge University Press.

Pérez Sobrino, P., Littlemore, J., & Houghton, D. (2019). The role of figurative complexity in the comprehension and appreciation of advertisements. *Applied Linguistics*, 40(6), 957–991.

Potter, R. F., & Bolls, P. D. (2012). *Psychophysiological Measurement and Meaning. Cognitive and Emotional Processing of Media*. New York: Routledge.

Pragglejaz Group. (2007). MIP: A method for identifying metaphorically used words in discourse. *Metaphor and Symbol*, 22(1), 1–39.

Purton, C. (2014). *The Trouble with Psychotherapy: Counselling and Common Sense*. London: Springer.

Quinn, N. (1991). The cultural basis of metaphor. In J. Fernandez, ed., *Beyond Metaphor: The Theory of Tropes in Anthropology*. Stanford: Stanford University Press, pp. 56–93.

Reise, S. P., Waller, N. G., & Comrey, A. L. (2000). Factor analysis and scale revision. *Psychological Assessment*, 12(3), 287–297.

Revicki, D. A., Cook, K. F., Amtmann, D., Harnam, N., Chen, W. H., & Keefe, F. J. (2014). Exploratory and confirmatory factor analysis of the PROMIS pain quality item bank. *Quality of Life Research*, 23(1), 245–255.

Riley, A. H., Critchlow, E., Birkenstock, L. et al. (2021). Vignettes as research tools in global health communication: A systematic review of the literature from 2000 to 2020. *Journal of Communication in Healthcare*, 14(4), 283–292.

Robinson, J. W., Herman, A., & Kaplan, B. J. (1982). Autonomic responses correlate with counselor-client empathy. *Journal of Counseling Psychology*, 29(2), 195–198.

Rogers, C. R. (1986). A client-centered/person-centered approach to therapy. In I. Kutash & A. Wolfe, eds., *Psychotherapist's Casebook*. New York: Jossey-Bass, pp. 197–208.

Röhricht, F. (2009). Body-oriented psychotherapy: The state of the art in empirical research and evidence based practice: A clinical perspective. *Body, Movement and Dance in Psychotherapy*, 4(2), 135–156.

Rosenbaum, M., & Ronen, T. (1998). Clinical supervision from the standpoint of cognitive-behaviour therapy. *Psychotherapy*, 35(2), 220–230.

Sarpavaara, H., & Koski-Jännes, A. (2013). Change as a journey: Clients' metaphoric change talk as an outcome predictor in initial motivational sessions with probationers. *Qualitative Research in Psychology*, 10(1), 86–101.

Semino, E., Demjén, Z., Hardie, A., Payne, S., & Rayson, P. (2018). *Metaphor, Cancer, and the End of Life. A Corpus-Based Study*. New York: Routledge.

Sensky, T., Turkington, D., Kingdon, D. et al. (2000). A randomized controlled trial of cognitive-behavioral therapy for persistent symptoms in schizophrenia resistant to medication. *Archives of General Psychiatry*, 57(2), 165–172.

Sims, P. A. (2003). Working with metaphor. *American Journal of Psychotherapy*, 57(4), 528–536.

Sims, P. A., & Whynot, C. A. (1997). Hearing metaphor: An approach to working with family-generated metaphor. *Family Process*, 36, 341–355.

Spong, S. (2010). Discourse analysis: Rich pickings for counsellors and therapists. *Counselling and Psychotherapy Research*, 10(1), 67–74.

Star, K. L., & Cox, J. A. (2008). The use of phototherapy in couples and family counseling. *Journal of Creativity in Mental Health*, 3(4), 373–382.

Steen, G. (2011). The contemporary theory of metaphor: Now new and improved! *Review of Cognitive Linguistics*, 9(1), 26–64.

Steen, G., Dorst, A., Herrmann, J. B. et al. (2010). *A Method for Linguistic Metaphor Identification: From MIP to MIPVU*. Amsterdam: John Benjamins.

Stevanovic, M., Tuhkanen, S., Järvensivu, M. et al. (2021). Physiological responses to proposals during dyadic decision-making conversations. *PLOS ONE*, 16(1), e0244929.

Stevens, R., & Spears, E. H. (2009). Incorporating photography as a therapeutic tool in counseling. *Journal of Creativity in Mental Health*, 4(1), 3–16.

Stott, R., Mansell, W., Salkovskis, P., Lavender, A., & Cartwright-Hatton, S. (2010). *Oxford Guide to Metaphors in CBT. Building Cognitive Bridges.* Oxford: Oxford University Press.

Tay, D. (2011). THERAPY IS A JOURNEY as a discourse metaphor. *Discourse Studies*, 13(1), 47–68.

Tay, D. (2012). Applying the notion of metaphor types to enhance counseling protocols. *Journal of Counseling & Development*, 90(2), 142–149.

Tay, D. (2013). *Metaphor in Psychotherapy. A Descriptive and Prescriptive Analysis.* Amsterdam: John Benjamins.

Tay, D. (2014). An analysis of metaphor hedging in psychotherapeutic talk. In M. Yamaguchi, D. Tay, & B. Blount, eds., *Approaches to Language, Culture, and Cognition.* Basingstoke: Palgrave MacMillan, pp. 251–267.

Tay, D. (2015). Metaphor in case study articles on Chinese university counseling service websites. *Chinese Language and Discourse*, 6(1), 28–56.

Tay, D. (2016a). A variational approach to deliberate metaphors. *Cognitive Linguistic Studies*, 3(2), 278–299.

Tay, D. (2016b). Finding the middle ground between therapist-centred and client-centred metaphor research in psychotherapy. In M. O'Reilly & J. N. Lester, eds., *The Palgrave Handbook of Adult Mental Health.* London: Palgrave Macmillan, pp. 558–576.

Tay, D. (2016c). Metaphor and psychological transference. *Metaphor and Symbol*, 31(1), 11–30.

Tay, D. (2017a). Quantitative metaphor usage patterns in Chinese psychotherapy talk. *Communication & Medicine*, 14(1), 51–68.

Tay, D. (2017b). The nuances of metaphor theory for constructivist psychotherapy. *Journal of Constructivist Psychology*, 30(2), 165–181.

Tay, D. (2017c). Time series analysis of discourse. A case study of metaphor in psychotherapy sessions. *Discourse Studies*, 19(6), 694–710.

Tay, D. (2017d). Exploring the metaphor–body–psychotherapy relationship. *Metaphor and Symbol*, 32(3), 178–191.

Tay, D. (2017e). Using metaphor in healthcare: Mental health. In E. Semino & Z. Demjén, eds., *Routledge Handbook of Metaphor and Language.* New York: Routledge, pp. 371–385.

Tay, D. (2020a). Affective engagement in metaphorical versus literal communication styles in counseling. *Discourse Processes*, 57(4), 360–375.

Tay, D. (2020b). Metaphor in mental healthcare [special issue]. *Metaphor and the Social World*, 10(2).

Tay, D. (2020c). Surveying views of metaphor vs. Literal language in psychotherapy: A factor analysis. *Metaphor and the Social World*, 10(2), 273–291.

Tay, D. (2020d). A computerized text and cluster analysis approach to psychotherapy talk. *Language & Psychoanalysis*, 9(1), 1–22.

Tay, D., Huang, J., & Zeng, H. (2019). Affective and discursive outcomes of symbolic interpretations in picture-based counseling: A skin conductance and discourse analytic study. *Metaphor and Symbol*, 34(2), 96–110.

Tay, D., & Neimeyer, R. A. (2021). Making meaning with metaphor in grief therapy. *Cognitive Linguistic Studies*, 8(1), 151–173.

Tay, D., & Qiu, H. (2022). Modeling linguistic (a)synchrony: A case study of therapist–client interaction. *Frontiers in Psychology*, 13, 903227 .

Tharp, R. G. (1999). Therapist as teacher: A developmental model of psychotherapy. *Human Development*, 42, 18–25.

Thompson, S. J., Bender, K., Lantry, J., & Flynn, P. M. (2007). Treatment engagement: Building therapeutic alliance in home-based treatment with adolescents and their families. *Contemporary Family Therapy*, 29(1–3), 39–55.

Törneke, N. (2017). *Metaphor in Practice. A Professional's Guide to Using the Science of Language in Psychotherapy*. Oakland,CA: New Harbinger.

Van Parys, H., & Rober, P. (2013). Micro-analysis of a therapist-generated metaphor referring to the position of a parentified child in the family. *Journal of Family Therapy*, 35(1), 89–113.

Wackers, D. Y. M., Plug, H. J., & Steen, G. J. (2021). "For crying out loud, don't call me a warrior": Standpoints of resistance against violence metaphors for cancer. *Journal of Pragmatics*, 174, 68–77.

Wan, W. (2014). Constructing and developing ESL students' beliefs about writing through metaphor. *Journal of Second Language Writing*, 23, 53–73.

Watts, S., Mackenzie, A., Thomas, C. et al. (2013). CBT for depression: A pilot RCT comparing mobile phone vs. computer. *BMC Psychiatry*, 13(1), 49.

Wickman, S. A., Daniels, M. H., White, L. J., & Fesmire, S. A. (1999). A "primer" in conceptual metaphor for counselors. *Journal of Counseling & Development*, 77, 389–394.

Wittig, J., & Davis, J. (2012). Circles outside the circle: Expanding the group frame through dance/movement therapy and art therapy. *Arts in Psychotherapy*, 39(3), 168–172.

Wohl, J. (1989). Integration of cultural awareness into psychotherapy. *American Journal of Psychotherapy*, 43, 343–355.

Yu, N. (1998). *The Contemporary Theory of Metaphor: A Perspective from Chinese*. Amsterdam: John Benjamins.

Zeng, H., Tay, D., & Ahrens, K. (2020). A multifactorial analysis of metaphors in political discourse: Gendered influence in Hong Kong political speeches. *Metaphor and the Social World*, 10(1), 141–168.

Funding

This work was supported by the HKSAR Research Grants Council [PolyU
156033/18H].

Cambridge Elements ☰

Cognitive Linguistics

About the Series

Cambridge Elements in Cognitive Linguistics aims to extend the theoretical and methodological boundaries of cognitive linguistics. It will advance and develop established areas of research in the discipline, as well as address areas where it has not traditionally been explored and areas where it has yet to become well-established.

Cambridge Elements ☰

Cognitive Linguistics

www.ingramcontent.com/pod-product-compliance
Ingram Content Group UK Ltd.
Pitfield, Milton Keynes, MK11 3LW, UK
UKHW020446010325
455719UK00008B/401